MENTAL ILLNESS

PROGRESS AND PROSPECTS

NUMBER 16

BAMPTON LECTURES IN AMERICA

Delivered at Columbia University 1965

ROBERT H. FELIX

MENTAL ILLNESS

PROGRESS AND PROSPECTS

COLUMBIA UNIVERSITY PRESS
NEW YORK AND LONDON 1967

Robert H. Felix is Dean of the School of Medicine,
St. Louis University

Library of Congress Catalog Card Number: 67-20278
Printed in the United States of America

CONTENTS

MENTAL ILLNESS

PROGRESS AND PROSPECTS

CHAPTER I

TOWARD MENTAL HEALTH

IN THE BEGINNING there was only ignorance, superstition, fear, and cruelty. The roots of mental illnesses in our world, and man's fear of them, stretch backward to the very beginnings of man's reign on earth. For as long as man can remember there have been those of his fellows afflicted with demons and devils or punished by spirits who caused behavior considered to be a deviation from the normal. Man has always attributed to the supernatural that which he could not otherwise explain. To primitive man most of the phenomena which today we consider commonplace were great mysteries, and these he explained as the work of gods and demons. He saw spirits in storms and lightning, in earthquakes, in clouds, in trees, in flowers, in birds, and in man. These spirits, which could be either good or evil, controlled his destinies for better or for worse. Primitive man, being in most ways no different from his modern counterpart, was quite willing to attribute success to his own ingenuity and efforts, but misfortune he blamed upon supernatural influences. Illness and death were not regarded as natural phenomena, and only as the nature of disease was understood could they be attributed to natural causes. Quite understandably, although the shades of ignorance rolled back, supernatural forces, or at least punishment for misbehavior, were credited with causing the still mysterious maladies.

Since spirits, good or evil, caused misfortune, disease, and death in the minds of primitive man, and since spirits or demons were at the root of many of the characteristics of mortal man, effort was made to neutralize their effect by promises, gifts, incantations, and rituals.

Approached through such logic, explanation of disease became simple and sweeping: it could be brought on by a good spirit or god as a punishment for sin or misdoing or as punishment for a slight or oversight, or it could be caused by an evil spirit or deity out of sheer malevolence, when the evil spirit as often inhabited the body as he influenced it through charms or spells.

Since all illness could be explained by such an hypothesis, it is small wonder that that most feared of illnesses, mental illness, was particularly thought to result from such influences. Since knowledge of this condition remained obscure long after physical conditions were at least partially understood, the concept of demonology has persisted until very recent times.

In the early ages of man a person so afflicted was often an object of hatred, fear, and rejection. To be sure, some of those so afflicted, whose illness or symptoms seemed to have a religious origin, were thought to be endowed by the gods with supernatural powers. But by and large, as in Egypt and early Greece, madness was considered as visited on mortals by angry, offended, or capricious gods. More often, when the response was unusual or different, the afflicted were deemed to be inhabited by evil spirits. He was often fortunate who only lost his life, for the cures devised to rid him of his demon or evil spirit were far more fearful than death.

From the cloudy days of early history to the enlightened days of our own generation is really but a step in time, but the advances that have been made to improve the plight of the mentally ill have been gradual ones, and only during the past two or three decades have they come with understanding and determination.

The story of mental illness is part of the larger story of man's growing awareness of his environment and of his responsibilities as a social animal. Development of a social consciousness was a necessary prerequisite, but even then understanding and determination were painfully slow in coming for the mentally afflicted.

In prehistoric times man's approach to management of the bizarre behavior of a mentally ill person, proceeding as it did from the premise that the victim was controlled by an evil spirit, was based on the objective of getting the demon out of the host. The unfortunate one might have his skull trephined to enable the spirit to escape through the resulting access to the outside world. Or medicine men might perform rites of exorcism, which could—and very often did—mean torture and great pain for the victim.

There have probably been some men in every age who tried their best to treat the mentally ill with humane compassion based on the belief that such conditions were due to natural causes. Asklepiades of Bithynia, who came to Rome in 91 B.C.,[1] was particularly interested in the mentally ill. He pioneered in humane treatment and discarded the earlier practice of confining mental patients in dark rooms. Instead he placed them in light, well-ventilated quarters, used occupational therapy, and prescribed exercises for improving the memory and occupying the patient. He, incidentally, employed two of nature's earliest tranquilizers, music and wine. Asklepiades made one of the earliest attempts at psychiatric classification, describing delusions, illusions, and hallucinations and considering them different types of illnesses.[2]

Caelius Aurelianus in the fourth century, A.D., who was considered the greatest physician after Galen, also gave much time and thought to the treatment of the mentally ill. Like Asklepiades, he also advocated rational and humane treatment and advised that patients be placed in well-lighted rooms. He insisted that attendants treat the patient with every consideration, and as a mode of treatment he employed hydrotherapy. He spoke severely against the use of fetters and flogging.[3] But others—in bitter fact, the majority for all succeeding centuries until the twentieth—have been fearful of what they did not understand and could not manage or control. What one fears he hates, and what one hates he tries to destroy by one means or another. It is small wonder then that the response not only of the average person but of the more enlightened segment of the population as well took the form of persecution and cruelty explained as rational and appropriate treatment.

Rendering the host inhospitable for the demon dwelling within was considered a logical way of cleansing the person of his demoniacal possession. Not only have those afflicted with mental illnesses been feared and hated, but those who have sought to help them by other than the accepted means have also been the object of society's wrath and fear. A classical example of this, together with a portrayal of the understanding of the concept of mental illness in that time, is to be found in the Bible in Luke VIII, 26th to 37th verses:

They came to the other side of the sea, to the country of the Gerasenes. And when He had come out of the boat, there met Him out of the tombs a man with an unclean spirit, who lived among the tombs; and no one could bind him any more, even with a chain; for he had often been bound with fetters and chains, but the chains he wrenched apart, and the fetters he broke in pieces; and no one had the strength to subdue him.

Night and day among the tombs and on the mountains he was always crying out, and bruising himself with stones. And when he saw Jesus from afar, he ran and worshipped Him; and crying out with a loud voice, he said, "What have you to do with me, Jesus, Son of the Most High God? I adjure you by God, do not torment me."

For He had said to him, "Come out of the man, you unclean spirit!"

And Jesus asked him "What is your name?" He replied, "My name is Legion; for we are many." And he begged Him eagerly not to send them out of the country. Now a great herd of swine was feeding there on the hillside; and they begged Him, "Send us to the swine; let us enter them." So He gave them leave.

And the unclean spirits came out, and entered the swine; and the herd, numbering about two thousand, rushed down the steep bank into the sea, and were drowned in the sea.

The herdsmen fled, and told it in the city and in the country. And people came to see what it was that had happened. And they came to Jesus, and saw the demoniac sitting there, clothed and in his right mind, the man who had had the legion; and they were afraid. And those who had seen it told what had happened to the demoniac and to the swine. And they began to beg Jesus to depart from their neighborhood.

So Jesus was forced to leave. The demoniac was an outcast, unable to hold a place in organized society. His fellow citizens had attempted to restrain his unnatural actions by fettering him or binding him with chains. When Jesus relieved him of his malady, the people who were watching did not rejoice in the cure, though they saw the man sitting clothed and in his right mind—rather they looked at Jesus and saw a mysterious power they could not understand. Thus the benefactor, too, became not a man to be praised but to be avoided, for he made those present uncomfortable. To many who have devoted themselves to helping the mentally ill, this may have a familiar ring.

What happened to the demoniac in his years before the day he met The Man From Nazareth has happened across the years—the mentally ill have been inexorably bound to their infirmities, and often they have been bound with chains. The treatment of the madman in the story from the Bible was no exception; he was one of the countless number of victims of society's fear and distrust of the unknown. The Nazarene was the exception in the way He treated the man. He was one of the few of His day with compassion, understanding, and courage.

Few though they may have been, some here and there through the centuries have lighted the path for those who followed after. One of these was the great physician of Antiquity, Hippocrates of Cos,[4] known as the Father of Medicine, who created the basis for the rational and scientific treatment of diseases, including mental diseases. Among the great contributions of Hippocrates which placed him among the giants of medicine was his removal from medicine of much of its supernatural trappings, even though the full effect of this was not to be felt for centuries to come. Hippocrates argued that mental illness was not the result of some supernatural possession but rather that it proceeded from natural causes.

Discussing epilepsy, which was also a condition of unknown etiology and which was commonly known as the "sacred disease," Hippocrates stated: "The 'sacred disease' appears to me to be nowise more divine nor more sacred than other diseases; but has a natural cause from which it originates like other affections. Men regard its nature and cause as divine from ignorance and wonder because it is not at all like other diseases." His attitude toward mental illnesses was similar. In speaking about cure of mental diseases by rites of purification and incantation, he said: "They who first attributed this disease to the gods seemed to me to have been just such persons as the conjurors, purificators, mountebanks, and charlatans now are."

Hippocrates advocated the use of decency and understanding in handling the mentally ill who, he said, were amenable to treatment, stressing natural causes and brain pathology, a concept he based upon clinical observation. Although some of his observations would by no means be considered completely accurate today, his remarkable logic in arriving at his conclusions laid the groundwork for what came later. In speaking of emotions, both normal and pathological, he said: "Men ought to know that from nothing else but the brain come joy, despondency, and lamentation and by the same organ we become mad and delirious and fears and terrors assail us, some by night and some by day."

He was the first of a number of outstanding men during the Golden Age of Greece to use gentleness and kindness with the mentally ill. Although Hippocrates was limited in his knowledge of the anatomy and physiology of the human body, since the Greek deification of the human body made dissection impossible, his concept went far beyond that of the people who believed in demon possession or control by evil spirits.

In the Golden Age of Greece others than the Father of Medicine expressed themselves on the subject of mental diseases. Among these were Plato and Aristotle,[5] neither of them often associated in men's minds with mental illness. Plato expressed the belief that persons with emotional disturbances were not responsible for their acts; centuries ahead of his time he advocated humane treatment for the sufferers in their own communities. Aristotle rejected psychological causes for mental illness, holding that man's mind is independent and immortal, and thus incapable of being diseased. Mental disturbances, he said, reflected organic impairment of the mind.

In spite of the types of treatment recommended by these three—advanced far beyond the tortures and restraints imposed on the mentally ill by others of their age—their beliefs actually had a retarding effect upon many aspects of the study of the mind. Psychological implications were discounted or ignored; this meant that studies and developments for adequate psychological treatment of the mentally ill were so rare as to be almost nonexistent.

Still, the ideas of pleasant surroundings, gentle treatment, and therapeutic activities persisted in some quarters, particularly in the Egyptian city of Alexandria, in a few Greek cities, and, later, in Rome.[6]

Aretaeus the Cappadocian,[7] who lived in the second century A.D., indicated that mental illness was an extension of normal thought processes. He described the relationship between mania and melancholia, thereby being the first to describe these conditions as parts of one type of illness. Thus was manic-depressive psychosis anticipated two thousand years before Kraeplin so classified the disease. The prevailing thought in Aretaeus' time was that mania was a condition which developed in people who were excitable and violent in action, while depression was an ailment of moody, serious people. Aretaeus' concept that each was a manifestation of the same illness was a radical departure for his day.

This light of antiquity which shone into the world of

the mentally ill was soon to be put out, but there is a final Roman who merits mention before the darkness falls. Galen,[8] in the second century A.D., did much in separating the mental illnesses into those with mental causes and those with physical causes. But with the death of Galen came the return to darkness, as superstition and unreason swept aside any remnants of the thinking of the early enlightened physicians.

Paradoxically, the spread of Christianity following the collapse of Greek and Roman civilizations closely paralleled the reversion to demonology that characterized the Dark Ages. Man was deemed to be simply a pawn in the supernatural hands of the demons and spirits who fought for his soul. And again the idea became prevalent that illness, particularly mental illness, was a punishment delivered by a displeased God.

At least one physician took exception to this commonly held concept. Johannes Actuarius,[9] or as he was sometimes known, Johannes son of Zacharias, a court physician at Constantinople during the latter part of the thirteenth century, wrote a work on "Functions and Disturbances on the Soul Spirit" in which he pointed out the dependence of mental symptoms on bodily causes, dietary errors, intemperance, and fatigue, and advised diets, baths, and exercise for these patients. Unfortunately this was the age of demoniacal possession, and the rational and humane advice of Johannes fell upon the deaf ears of contemporaries who saw mental disease only as the work of evil spirits.

The Middle Ages—a dark period of ignorance, fear,

and depression—may be one more point in the argument for environment as an important contributing factor in the etiology of mental illnesses. If one can credit what history has passed on to us, there may have been more such illness during these centuries than in ancient times. There was the appearance of hysterias—such as the dancing mania known as St. Vitus' Dance—which on occasion affected almost entire communities. This condition was described by Paracelsus [10] in his monograph on "Diseases that Deprive Man of His Reason," an early classic on mental diseases. Paracelsus also described mania and several other conditions. There were the spreading beliefs in lycanthropy and vampirism. There was the Children's Crusade. Madness seemed to prevail everywhere.[11]

The oppression of men who were not allowed to exercise any form of freedom, who were kept ignorant and uneducated, and who were forced to live in poverty and squalor had the effect of intensifying and broadening the superstitions that were the foundations of demonology. During the early years of the Middle Ages the mentally ill were cared for by the priests, who had assumed many of the physicians' functions in a way that bespoke their priestly calling.

At first exorcism of spirits was done gently, with such rites as laying on of hands, prayer, and visits to places considered holy; but gradually men concluded that demons and spirits were in league with the devil, heaven's original outcast. It was pride that had caused the devil's downfall, and an insult to his pride was considered the way through which he and his minions could be driven out. Exorcistic rites thus became to a greater and greater extent punishment of the devil within the sick man, and little thought was given to the man himself. For of what good could a man be if he continued to be possessed; and how better could one discourage the devil in possession than to humiliate and make inhospitable the body where he had chosen to dwell?

By the fifteenth century this type of thinking reached its greatest intensity. There were two trains of thought that had evolved: first, the demon-possessed person was being punished by God for his sins; second, such a person had actually gone so far as to join with the devil voluntarily, selling his immortal soul for some reward in this world. This, it will be remembered, is the theme of *Faust*. There was no place for the thought that the mentally ill might simply be victims of illnesses whose causes were no more the fault of those afflicted than the victims of any other diseases.

Those in league with the devil were said to have signed pacts with him, and in exchange for their souls were given a number of supernatural powers with which they could control both the elements and their fellow men. They could cause floods and epidemics, they could inflict injury on others, they could fly through the air—they were witches. (Is it any wonder the mentally ill were feared, loathed, and avoided? Is it any wonder their condition stigmatized their entire family?)

It is difficult for most of us in the twentieth century to understand the attitudes of men or the condition of society at the time Columbus first sailed west. We have only to refer to any history of medicine to verify that the situation then was as described here. In terms of our present "enlightened" state, and I use the word advisedly, it would be easier to accept the fact that these conditions were prevalent if it could be explained as the attitude of the poor, the ignorant, and the uneducated but the fact is that leaders in theology, government officials, philosphers, and physicians of the time did more to promulgate the beliefs than did the common man, whose influence was practically nonexistent.

Even the Vatican lent its authority to what grew to be one of the most tragic movements in mankind's history. At the close of the fifteenth century Pope Innocent VIII issued a Bull in which he encouraged the hunt for witches, and unintentionally opened the way for persecution, harassment, torture, and death of many innocent people.[12]

Following the publication of the Bull, seeking out and eliminating witches became a religious duty as well as a commendable social act. Justification for the persecution of these poor creatures was found in Exodus XXII, 18th verse, which states "Thou shalt not suffer a witch to live." It will never be known how many innocent lives of the mentally ill and others as well were sacrificed through the literal adoption of this text. Certainly not less than a hundred thousand souls were executed as witches between the middle of the fifteenth century and the end of the seventeenth, which was the period of most horrible persecution. It is said that "twenty thousand witches" were burned or otherwise executed in Scotland alone during the seventeenth century, and unknown thousands were put to death in England, France, Germany, and elsewhere in Europe. It is known that 500 were burned at the stake in Geneva in a three-month period in the year 1515.[13]

The historian Lecky [14] describes the period thus:

> Never was the power of imagination . . . more strikingly evinced. Superstitious and terror-stricken, the minds of men were impelled irresistibly toward the miraculous and the Satanic, and they found them upon every side. The elements of imposture blended so curiously with the elements of delusion, that it is now impossible to separate them. . . . Madness is always peculiarly frequent during great religious and political revolutions; and in the Sixteenth Century all its forms were absorbed in the system of witchcraft and caught the color of the prevailing predisposition.

Methods of extracting confessions grew more and more radical. The truth is that a person selected for accusation had little chance of escape. Under torture, if it were intense enough and it almost always was, the most innocent person could be expected to confess.

Much of this was not aimed directly at the mentally ill, except that with their aberrations and their delusions or hallucinations they were often the first to be victimized. Inadvertently they helped spread the movement because many psychotic persons—even as today—believed they were influenced by malevolent forces, had committed unpardonable sins, or had actually signed pacts with the devil. Thus they readily confessed in the hope for relief, a relief they found only too often in death. That death was often a horrible one, for a person convicted as a witch faced beheading, strangling, mutilation, or burning—or any combination of these.

The movement gained momentum throughout Europe but reached its full terrible magnitude in the American Colonies in the sixteenth and seventeenth centuries when many hundreds of people were convicted and executed as witches.

For a time—and to thousands that time must have seemed interminable—it appeared as if torture, persecution, and death were to be the inevitable treatment accorded the mentally ill. In fact it was often worth one's life to offer the theory that people suffering with mental disturbances were sick people. But the intensity of practices surrounding the reactions to demonology demanded from some men that, no matter what the consequences, they must speak out and do whatever possible to change the situation. Among these men were Paracelsus, mentioned above, Johann Weyer, and Reginald Scot, but these men and others like them were hounded and vilified for their writings and actions.

Paracelsus [15] called for the type of treatment that would cure the mentally ill who, he said, were "our brothers." He ridiculed the notion of demoniacal possession, saying,

> Mental Diseases have nothing to do with either spirits or devils; the individuals who are mentally sick merely drink more of the "astral wine" than they can assimilate. The experienced doctor should not study how to exorcise the devil,

but rather how to cure the insane. . . . Let us give them treatment to cure them, for nobody knows whom among our friends and relatives this misfortune may strike.

Weyer[16] attempted to remove the stigma from witches by holding in contrast to what was maintained in *The Witch Hammer*,[17] a manual dealing with witches, that they were mentally sick, certainly not in league with the devil. He maintained that the possessed were blameless and entitled to sympathetic treatment and it was the demon who should be punished. Scot,[18] in his book *The Discovery of Witches*, also stressed the sickness of persons with mental disturbances. He laid bare and ridiculed the trappings and ritual of witchcraft and maintained that many of those who were accused of this black art needed, instead of chastisement, relief from disease.

In spite of the refutation and vilification men such as this underwent, the works they began could hardly fail to bear some fruit. One of the first steps, though at the time it could hardly have been called an advance, was the establishment of places where the mentally ill could be brought together, other than in the madhouses, jails, and workhouses which had been used as places of restraint so that the community could be protected. These places of refuge acquired the name of asylum, for while the inmates could be removed from the community and the primary concern was for the good of the community, there had begun to creep in, if only incidentally, concern for the welfare of the mentally ill person also.

One of the first of these asylums was the monastery of

St. Mary of Bethlehem in London, which was made officially into a mental hospital by Henry VIII. The London hospital's name was soon contracted to Bedlam, a term that came to mean noise, confusion, disorder, and purposeless behavior, the type of activity one envisioned when he thought of a mental hospital. Bedlam rapidly lost its original purpose and became notorious for the manner in which its inmates were treated and for the practices that went on there. Some of the more disturbed and bizarre patients, if they could be called patients, were put on public display; tractable ones were allowed outside to beg for the food that kept them alive.

Other asylums were established in other countries across the world but for the most part they were more concentrations of people still under the stigma of ignorance, superstition, and moral condemnation than havens of refuge and institutions of healing. Not until the eighteenth century did reform for the mentally ill actually become a movement with meaning. And then the movement was not an isolated one—it was part of a larger reform brought about by the Enlightenment, which showed other evidence of a social conscience such as prison reform, improvement of public health, and changes in the care of children.

All these changes, though slow in coming to fruition, were inevitable. Man had experienced the darkness of the Middle Ages and found enlightenment more to his liking. He began to rebel against those ideas and concepts as well as those individuals who held him in thrall. In the air were the winds of revolution, risen after the period of great exploration. Subservience had been tried as a way of life, but the man who had been subservient decided he was able to rule himself and his destiny as well as, and probably better than, many of those who had ruled him.

These winds of revolution pervaded every corner of the civilized world; for some people they would freshen quickly after the beginning of the last half of the eighteenth century; for others, such as the mentally ill, no more than faint breezes would stir for many decades yet to come. However, the faint stirrings presaged the final arrival of the winds of change.

They were few, to be sure, and often years apart. After St. Mary of Bethlehem came asylums in Mexico, 1566; in France, 1641; in Russia, 1764; in Vienna, 1784. In this country—still English colonies—the Pennsylvania Hospital in Philadelphia, with Benjamin Franklin playing an instrumental role, opened its doors to the mentally disturbed in 1756 and provided some wards for them. The first hospital in this country operated exclusively for the mentally ill was opened in Williamsburg, Virginia, in 1773.[19]

Even in these asylums, however, treatment was not much changed. Albert Deutsch in his great book *The Mentally Ill in America* described American treatment this way:

> Patient's scalps were shaved and blistered; they were bled to the point of syncope; purged until the alimentary canal failed to yield anything but mucus; and in the intervals, they were chained by the waist or ankle to the cell wall.[20]

Reaction to such treatment, and much worse, led William Tuke, an Englishman and a member of the Society of Friends, to establish York Retreat in 1792.[21] Tuke, incensed at the handling of inmates in York Asylum which had been opened some fifteen years earlier, made the York Retreat more of a hostel for the mentally ill, where they were treated with common sense based on humanitarian principles. The patients were allowed to work and to rest in a quiet environment; only the most disturbed were held in restraint.

Tuke's retreat directly influenced work with the mentally ill in the United States in the closing years of the eighteenth and in the early nineteenth centuries. Following the example set at York, the Friends' Asylum opened in Frankford, Pennsylvania in 1817 and the Bloomingdale Asylum opened in New York in 1821. In both places, treatment was humane, kind, and temperate.

Meanwhile, across the English Channel from York a French physician, lately given charge of the Bicêtre in Paris where mentally ill male patients were housed, proposed a radical change in the treatment, management, and care of patients which later came to be known as "Moral Treatment." This physician, Philippe Pinel,[22] was a brilliant student and had become particularly attracted to the problems and plight of the mentally ill. He had read extensively in the early literature, which had been largely forgotten by the then modern workers. He was both familiar and in agreement with the attitude of such early proponents of kindly treatment as Asklepiades, Aretaeus, Caelius Aurelianus, and others. He was convinced that the position of these ancients was much more sound therapeutically than what was then being done, so that it was not only desirable as an effective method of treatment but much more humane.

One French official, when he had heard what was proposed, remarked that Pinel must be mad himself. Pinel literally took his life in his hands when he unchained fifty-three mental patients at Bicêtre. Had their reaction been different he might well have lost his own head—under the blade of the guillotine that had come into recent favor during the French Revolution. But the patients, and some of them had been chained in dungeons for as many as thirty years, reacted positively to Pinel's positive treatment. Today it is axiomatic that patients so react; in Pinel's time to attempt such treatment was an act of uncommon courage.

Pinel later became physician for the Salpêtrière Hospital in Paris, where he again did away with chains and restraints. The effect was remarkable, and the stale, lifeless air that had surrounded the mentally ill for so many centuries began to lighten and the first whisper of the breeze of a new day began to waft across continents. Soon ten additional mental hospitals, based on Pinel's type of care, had been established across France.

In England, asylums, in the real meaning of the word, came into being under the County Asylum Act of 1808. The first such county institution established under the Act was that at Nottingham, which opened in 1811.[23]

Not only were care and treatment improved in these institutions, but the development of professional standards and a medical basis for the procedures instituted began to receive the attention they deserved. Europe was in the forefront of what has been called the first great psychiatric revolution, with Pinel as its leader. But in America the movement also grew swiftly and meaningfully.

Benjamin Rush, "The Father of American Psychiatry" and a signer of the Declaration of Independence, joined the staff of Philadelphia's Pennsylvania Hospital in 1783. He too called for more humane treatment of the mentally ill, although himself not entirely free of the shackles of superstition and the remnants of demonology. Rush used the popular methods of bleeding, restraints, and purgatives, but he used them in the spirit of attempting to provide real help for his patients. His use of these methods was entirely without the deliberate cruelty and brutality that earlier had been aimed at crushing the victim's "demon" or "devil." [24]

At this time in the United States such treatment as that at the Pennsylvania Hospital was, with few exceptions, available only to the well-to-do, who alone could afford it. The poor were considered to be the responsibility of their community, which did its best to discharge its responsibility. Unfortunately, with little understanding and even less knowledge, communities classed the mentally ill with the aged and the orphaned, lumped them all together under the term paupers, and treated them as criminals.

Some communities, where it was possible, put such creatures in poorhouses; but, with a lack of funds, facilities, and physicians, other communities were forced to put them in jails. In a number of early American towns they were even auctioned off, driven out of town, or sent to almshouses.

Undoubtedly in the beginning most communities wanted to discharge properly their responsibility, but within a rapidly growing United States men had, they thought, more pressing responsibilities. With the best they had at hand they did what they could for their ailing fellows, but the nation was young, lusty, and growing, and there was not much time to be spared for the misfits and incompetents. Besides, money was not a plentiful commodity and had to be put where it would count most, and very little was known about the cause or treatment of mental illnesses.

The mentally ill were thus shunted aside, given the least costly care, and placed where they were unable to be heard if they cried out against their treatment. As these places, mostly prisons, poorhouses, and madhouses, grew in size, there were Americans with social consciences who began to speak for those whose voices could not be heard.

Most persistent among these was a young schoolteacher who had been forced to give up her career because of physical illness. Dorothea Lynde Dix,[25] twenty years before the War Between the States, decided to fill her life with those activities that she was able to pursue. One of such activities was teaching a Sunday-school class for women in a prison. What she saw astonished her, for she found numberless mental patients mingled with the criminals, and she began to look into the conditions in which the mentally ill of her day found themselves. She discovered chains, fetters, inhuman beatings, unsanitary dungeon-like cells, deplorable crowding, woefully inadequate diets, neglect, abandonment by society.

Unlike most women of her day, Miss Dix saw a task of national moment that had to be done; and she set out to achieve it on a nationally effective scale. She wrote to members of the Congress of the United States, she visited institutions and hospitals across the country, she talked to newspaper writers, she aroused public opinion, she goaded state legislatures. She succeeded.

Miss Dix was instrumental in the creation of the first federal hospital for the insane, St. Elizabeth's in Washington, D.C.; and before her death in 1887 she was directly responsible for the founding of a total of thirty-two mental hospitals in the United States.

One of her greatest personal accomplishments was the passage of a bill by Congress in 1854 setting aside a total of more than ten million acres of Federal land to be used for land grants to the states to provide for the indigent mentally ill. The idea behind the bill was the same as that of the college land-grant legislation, which meant so much in the establishment of state colleges across the country.

Although the bill was vetoed by President Franklin Pierce, the work that had been done by Miss Dix was well started and became a part of the American conscience. A new future seemed to be in store for the mentally ill.

The system worked well initially; the early successes were a result of state action in providing for the people where community resources were inadequate. It was a combined effort in each state, and the hospitals were most often situated in rural settings where their patients could be protected from the stresses of urban life and could hopefully recover, or failing that, could live out their lives in a peaceful, pastoral type of institutional existence.

But these seeds of humanitarianism contained their own bitter fruit. The hospital provided a place where a disturbed and disturbing incompetent citizen could be sent to prevent him from creating too great a burden for his family and for his neighbors. Unsure what to do with a person whose actions were not criminal but were yet not normal, communities sent him to the mental hospital. And gradually hospital populations began to grow. New developments in the treatment of illnesses, developments which made so many tremendous advances during the nineteenth century, nevertheless had not yet included the mental illnesses, and in many cases there was little that could be done for a patient other than tend to his needs and make him as comfortable as possible.

The drawback in this situation was that the hospital was a finite entity. It could hold only a certain number of patients—rather, it was built to hold that certain number. But when patients came they stayed, and more and more of them came and stayed until death provided release. Hospital facilities were filled, became crowded, and then overcrowded. Mental illnesses for the most part were sicknesses with but one outcome—hospitalization—long, long years of hospitalization.

Even the treatments that had been attempted during those early years became impossible to achieve when the case load of a physician was so overwhelming that there was no time even to speak to a patient every day. These frustrations were magnified by the now gloomy atmosphere of the outmoded buildings, the lack of assistance, the shortages of medical equipment, the inadequate budgets.

As the nineteenth century drew to a close, there were those who would have done something to alleviate the bleak outlook if they could. But communities, which had tried and failed years before in their efforts to care for their own mentally ill, were lulled by the knowledge that their neighbors were being cared for by the state.

All was not dark, however. Benjamin Rush and Dorothea Lynde Dix, among others, had heralded the inevitable but still unseen dawn of a new day. Medicine was beginning to rise above its witch-doctor beginnings. Psychiatry grew—to a great degree separately, but it grew. In 1844 a group of medical superintendents of mental institutions formed the organization that was the forerunner of the American Psychiatric Association. At the close of the century, a young man named Clifford Beers was wrestling with the torments of his mind, and those torments would soon send him to a mental hospital. In Europe Sigmund Freud was starting his life's work. His "Studies on Hysteria" with Joseph Breuer was published in 1895. It was the time for the emergence of psychiatry. Nina Ridenhour has said in her excellent book, *Mental Health in the United States:* [26]

> Historians of psychiatry date its emergence from institutional isolation variously from 1900 to 1914, but they all agree that up until then psychiatry *had* been isolated and that it *did* emerge. Many forces entered into bringing about the emergence. Among them: the growing population of the United States with correspondingly greater numbers of the mentally ill; the turn of the century as a period of social reform, and increasing public acceptance of social responsibility; the growth of the scientific method and important new medical discoveries; improved medical schools resulting in better medical and psychiatric training; the new ideas of the period, especially the concept of psychogenesis; and, not least, the recognition of psychiatry's "practical usefulness."

The Western World was moving toward better mental health practices, though it had yet to coin the term to describe a movement that would involve millions of interested citizens, as well as two Presidents of the United States. The new era was ahead, but the foundations upon which it would be built would take at least another half century and two world-wide wars to complete.

CHAPTER II

AN AROUSED AMERICA

AS WORLD WAR II drew to a close in 1945, the American people became aware of a problem the size and scope of which had not been suspected but which had had an impact on this nation's war effort and would have to be reckoned with in the postwar years ahead. While only gradually perceived during the early months and years of the war, the effect was cumulative, and at war's end came the realization that psychiatric impairment had seriously crippled American military strength.

In 1940 and 1941 the United States had gone about its business, hoping to the point of belief that the great conflict engulfing the rest of the world would not involve the Western Hemisphere. Within our castle surrounded by the world's largest moat—the Atlantic Ocean on one side and the Pacific on the other—we would be safe, secure, unassailable. We had started a draft of young men for military service in 1940, but it was more to fortify our feeling of security at home than to build a great fighting machine. We were assured by many of the most important men of the time that Hitler wanted no expanded war, that the Japanese aggressions in the Far East posed no threats to us. In addition, we Americans felt secure in the belief that, if anything did happen to involve us, our strength was such that we could make short work of any aggressor.

What happened in the last month of 1941 is, of course, a well-known matter of history. But when we lost most of our Pacific fleet in the attack on Pearl Harbor, when we realized that our commitments would stretch so far in two directions from our continental position that they would nearly girdle the globe, and when we learned that the fighting abilities and machines of our enemies were so formidable—then we saw that the days of war stretched far ahead of us. To gain victory meant mobilization on a breathtaking scale hitherto undreamed by us. Always in such circumstances manpower is the primary concern. The draft was intensified and American youth by the millions were screened to find those fit young men necessary to build the armed force that was required to overcome our enemies and bring us victory.

In the course of this sifting process, essential in the waging of any war, it was dismaying to learn how many of our young men had emotional disabilities which disqualified them for service. Between January 1942 and June 1945, according to W. C. Menninger,[1] out of approximately 15 million examinations for inductions into the Armed Services, 1,875,000 individuals were rejected for neuropsychiatric disability. To put it another way, for every 100 men examined, 12 were rejected for neuropsychiatric reasons. This figure rose from 9.7 per 100 in 1942 to 16.4 per 100 in 1945. For every 100 rejections for all causes, neuropsychiatric rejections accounted for 39.1 for the years 1942 through 1945. This proportion rose from a low of 28.4 in 1942 to a high of 45.8 in 1944.

These figures represented the loss at induction. Considering for a moment only the Army, of those who entered and subsequently received a Certificate of Disability discharge for any cause whatsoever, 37 per cent or 387,000 were discharged for neuropsychiatric conditions. All of this manpower loss, before and after induction, totaled more men than were assigned to the Pacific Theatre of Operations during the war.

If these young men were representative of the Nation as a whole, what would be the absolute figures for the mental and nervous impairments of the entire population? Certainly that proportion of our population between eighteen and forty-five years of age should represent the flower of our manhood. The prevalence of such disorders in the rest of the people was very likely no less. Our knowledge of the situation widened as spot studies which had been carried out were reported in the literature, and we were faced with a truer picture of America's mental health. The number of those afflicted, not merely those in hospitals, was larger than heretofore had been realized. At least one study projected the figure of one American in ten who needed psychiatric help of some kind; treatment facilities were in woefully short supply, state hospitals were overcrowded and understaffed; private treatment was long and expensive and beyond the reach of most Americans; and our therapeutic armamentarium was limited.

As a result of studies carried out in 1935 and 1936 an estimate of the prevalence of mental disorders in the civilian population was made by the United States Public Health Service, based on an enumeration made in a house-to-house canvass in selected, primarily urban, communities. All cases of disabling illness lasting a week or more were counted, and it was found that 549 per 100,000 of the population studied were suffering from an emotional disorder. Other estimates were made by other investigators which were much more sophisticated in nature and were based on a more refined research design. In the Eastern Health District of Baltimore, Maryland, Lemkau, Tietze, and Cooper studied the emotional problems prevalent during one year, 1936,[2] and reported a prevalence rate of 60.5 per 1,000 persons examined. This survey included adult delinquency as a mental disorder. In Williamson County, Tennessee, Roth and Luton [3] surveyed a population in 1938 which was primarily rural. Their survey was a one-day prevalence study, which means that they surveyed the amount of mental illness prevalent in the County on a single day, namely September 1, 1938. They reported 1,738 cases or a prevalence rate of 69.4 per 1,000 persons examined. While these two studies were not statistically comparable for a number of reasons such as differences in diagnostic categories employed and the time span of the studies, the results were amazingly close together. There were some figures available for the Nation as a whole also. The population of patients in public mental hospitals had been reported for many years.[4] In 1904 there were 183.6 patients in public mental hospitals per 100,000 of the general population. In 1910 this had risen to 204.2 per 100,000 and by 1923 the rate was 245 per 100,000. In 1950 a figure is reported for the number of patients in all hospitals for mental disorders, public and private, except veterans' hospitals. The rate that year was 412.6 per 100,000 of the general population. The incidence of mental disorders, that is, the rate of occurrence of new cases, as judged from first admissions to mental hospitals had risen through the years. The first year for which accurate data are available is 1922, when the rate of new admissions was 68.2 per 100,000 of the general population. This rose to 102.5 per 100,000 in 1950. According to the rates of first admissions in New York state alone in 1920, out of every 1,000 males born that year, 48.2 could be expected to be admitted to a mental hospital before the entire group had died out. This is equivalent to one out of every 20.7 individuals. For females, comparable figures for that year were 48.1 per 1,000 or one in 20.8. In 1930 this expectation had risen to 63.9 per 1,000 or one in 14.6, for males, and, for females, 55.8 per 1,000 or one in 17.9. In 1940 the expectation of mental illness at birth for males rose to 80.9 per 1,000 or one in 12.4 and, for females, 82.0 per 1,000 or one in 12.2.

Still the picture was not entirely dark. Many who understood the unhappy situation were laboring mightily to stimulate reforms. They had pleaded their cause with such vigor and such persuasion that many of the informed people of the country had become aware that we were facing a serious problem of national magnitude which must be solved and they were receptive to sound recommendations for reform. And this informed citizenry ranged from the ordinary citizen to the most powerful Congressman.

How had this come about? Why had the mental health movement, as it is called now, been as successful as it had during the half century since 1900?

Interestingly enough, these questions can be answered to a large extent with the name of one man—Clifford Beers, a businessman who wrote a book. Beers, the young man mentioned earlier who at the turn of the century was wrestling with the torments of his mind, was one of those people who have not wittingly been thrust into the midst of a movement, but one of those who once involved have accepted the charge given them. Beers was not a born crusader; rather, what happened to him came when the times were ready for him. People had begun to look at each other as people; where there was poverty, sordidness, injustice, disease, there must be ways to change these conditions for the better.

Broad social movements could count on support—some of it indifferent support, to be sure. But as the nineteenth century gave place to the twentieth, the cultural climate was such that an organized mental health movement could take seed and prosper. Swift industrialization and a rapid population expansion had produced a major social reordering. For society as a whole, these years brought a great deal more political and social involvement than in the past. They brought the growth of big business and the countering growth of big labor, along with unprecedented expansions in communities and individual interest that ranged far beyond the boundaries of the local community and the country. These years brought social welfare legislation, child labor laws, mental testing programs, suburbia, progressive education, the feminist movement, and a realignment of family life.

The turn of the century witnessed major medical advances that marked the beginning of an interdisciplinary approach to normal and maladaptive behavior. History was reinterpreted in the light of new knowledge of the body, the mind, the emotions, and society. Eugenic theory, discovery of the spirochete in the etiology of general paresis, the neuron theory, discoveries in physiology, chemistry, and bacteriology, the psychoanalytic psychology of Freud, Meyerian psychology, Adlerian and Jungian approaches to thought and behavior, and a newly evolved field of psychiatric social work—all this led to a hope based on accumulating evidence that many of the scourges of mankind could be controlled, if not eliminated.

Such was the climate in the United States when Clifford Beers, a native of New Haven, Connecticut, and a graduate of Yale University, found himself entering a mental hospital as a patient.

He arrived there as a result of a family misfortune. During his undergraduate years at Yale, his older brother was stricken with epilepsy. Beers, with no outward signs during his college days and afterward, was gnawed by the fear that he, too, was epileptic. In 1900, when he was but twenty-four years of age, the fear so overwhelmed him that he tried to commit suicide by plunging from the window of his fourth-floor room. Fortunately the attempt failed—and with his failure went the fear of epilepsy.

For that fear, however, he substituted delusions, ranging from feelings of persecution to those of grandeur. The next three years he spent in three mental institutions, where he ran the gamut of the treatments that were the order of that day. He ran head on into the concepts of mental illness that, based on the information available, then prevailed. While the dedicated personnel did their best for the mentally ill, the atmosphere in both private institutions and state-supported hospitals was one in which the patient was treated as something less than an equal human being. Beers was treated harshly by today's standards, confined alone for long periods in isolation, and was kept in a straitjacket. Although hospital officials and attendants were convinced that patients could not react normally, they nevertheless often dealt harshly with abnormal reactions.

After the first two years or so of hospitalization, Beers lost his feelings of persecution, but they were supplanted by pathological elation. But it was during this time that he began to formulate plans to improve the plight of the mentally ill. To document his thinking he began writing down his experiences; carefully he observed and recorded those things—some of them harsh, some of them brutal, some of them even worse—that happened to him and to his fellow patients.

In 1903 Beers left mental institutions. He re-entered the business world, where his difference from the people around him soon made itself felt in his thinking. Most people would have been happy to leave the dismal world of the mentally ill forever, counting themselves fortunate to be free.

Beers, however, though he felt fortunate, could not forget his experiences nor the resolve that he had made to find some way to help those who were not as fortunate as he. During his hospitalization he had dreamed of a world-wide mental health movement and that dream remained with him.

Casting about for a viable force that would make translation of his dream into reality a possibility, Beers remembered the impact that the novel *Uncle Tom's Cabin* had had in pushing the movement against slavery. He thought of his own writings and decided to redo them in the form of a book. He would not make the mistakes others had before him—for there had been a number of mental hospital exposés—but he would write a book based on fact, on good scientific opinion, on the need for action.

He took a leave of absence from his business to set his hand to the manuscript. From these endeavors emerged the classic *A Mind That Found Itself*.[5] Before the book was published in 1908 the manuscript had been reviewed and criticized by many leading physicians in psychiatry, by psychologists, and by other leaders of the day. Professor William James, the Harvard psychologist who at first told Beers he did not have time to read the manuscript but then changed his mind and did read it, became one of Beers' staunchest supporters, even writing the book's introduction.

At the same time the book was being prepared for the printer Beers was setting about translating his dream into action. He organized a group in New Haven in May, 1908, the Connecticut Society for Mental Hygiene—the first of a chain of such organizations and the pilot for a national organization. The National Committee for Mental Hygiene came into existence the next year. Beers had strong support and encouragement from Professor James and from Dr. Adolph Meyer, Henry Phipps Professor of Psychiatry at The Johns Hopkins University. It was Dr. Meyer who actually suggested the term "mental hygiene," although the phrase had been coined several decades earlier.

The National Committee, of which Beers served as secretary, was the forerunner of today's National Association for Mental Health, the national citizens' organization in the area of mental health.

For the first few years after the national movement began, improving mental hospital conditions was the primary concern of its members and of the public. This was logical and understandable since almost all care and treatment of the mentally ill was carried on in institutions. Any other treatment was essentially unknown and nonexistent. Institutional care had sunk to a low ebb, and any reforms in the care and treatment of the mentally ill had to begin with a change in procedures and attitude in the mental hospitals.

Then World War I interrupted much of the still-limited activity in this field; but it taught the health professions and the public a great deal about mental illnesses and the potential value of mental hygiene. The experiences of the war indicated that simply treating the mentally ill was not the sole aim of mental hygiene; preventive techniques were necessary. Just as with other illnesses and diseases, one of the important needs was for methods to halt successfully the beginnings of mental illnesses.

The war also had another effect: it introduced the psychological view of mental illnesses both to the scientific professions and the general public. Although the psychodynamics of hysteria and other disorders were known at the beginning of the war, most physicians, including psychiatrists, if not rejecting them outright, resisted acceptance of the psychological theories. But with "shell shock" incapacitating almost as many men as combat wounds, more and more of the medical officers came to admit that at least certain cases of mental illness required consideration of psychological factors.

A potent force which was influential in the acceptance of the concept that psychological factors played a causal role in the production of emotional disorders was the widespread use of intelligence testing in the screening of recruits. This was the first time such testing had been done, and as it came into wide use the concepts underlying these procedures became, to an increasing degree, incorporated into medical thinking.

After the war, however, interest first centered on providing services and facilities for maladjusted children. It was generally accepted that emotional disorders had their origins early in life. What better area then to concentrate efforts at prevention and treatment than with the young? It was immediately clear that the mental hospital was inappropriate as a treatment setting for children. The child's total environment—his home, his school, the agencies of the community in which he lived—had to be considered. Then the concern of courts, schools, welfare agencies, and other community elements led naturally from exclusive interest in mentally ill children to the concept of child guidance clinics. This movement became firmly established in 1922.

The most significant outcome of pioneering in child guidance was the stimulus it gave to mental health research. The genesis of mental illnesses now began to be sought in earnest, and the search led to the child's entire range of relationships. The identification of physical and emotional factors that contributed to disturbances in the individual child was followed by the identification of family and community factors that contributed to the child's personality development. The next step then followed inevitably; this was the recognition that there was a need for mental health services not for the child alone, but perhaps as urgently for his parents, his brothers and sisters, and all the others within his sphere who were responsible for or who influenced his growth and development, since their state of mental health had a profound effect on the mental health and emotional maturation of the child.

The contributions of the pioneers in the establishment of child guidance and adult clinics were not confined to additional health services for children and their parents. Indeed, they stressed the need for a new approach in the battles against mental illness, an approach based upon a balanced and integrated program of services and research.

The movement grew sporadically during the years of the 1920s although there was little organized leadership at the national level outside the National Committee for Mental Hygiene. Again, it was a time confined mostly to individual effort: here a psychiatrist would attempt and succeed at something new; there a hospital would find that humane treatment paid dividends in better results. But seemingly no matter how successful these isolated cases, communication was poor and there was seldom a concerted movement to adapt the successes on a broader scale.

Against such a background was born the Federal Government's interest in the problems of mental illness and its treatment. The government's involvement was based on the fundamental policy that it should not enter the state or local picture unless there was a national need, and attempts of individuals or groups could not be effective because of limitation of funds or authority. Even then it should confine itself to those areas where assistance was needed.

The first of these areas which the government entered had to do with the problems centering around admission of immigrants from foreign countries. Studies indicated a higher incidence of foreign-born among admissions to the mental hospitals of New York State than of any other group. The U.S. Public Health Service,[6] which had been established in 1798, was accordingly charged with the examination and medical certification of aliens as they arrived on American shores.

A more important impetus to a federal mental health program, however, came from what many people would consider another direction—and something of an unexpected direction at that. Following passage of the Harrison Narcotics Act in 1914, the cause or causes of narcotic addiction and its treatment and cure became a matter of serious concern to the medical profession and government alike. The number of addicts in the United States was not accurately known, but it was commonly thought that they were relatively numerous. These people required the drug to stave off withdrawal symptoms which could be severe, or even in some cases fatal. Yet there was a federal law against prescribing or dispensing these substances except for clearly defined medical reasons. And narcotic addiction, now recognized as a medical condition, was not then so considered by the majority of people.

The more the phenomena making up the complex

known as narcotic drug addiction were studied, the more it became apparent that this was a psychological and social as well as a biological problem. Because of the stigma which had become attached to narcotic addiction, a result of the publicity it had received, and because of the manner in which the legislation was interpreted and enforced, this was not a popular area for bright and able physicians and investigators to enter. They were viewed with suspicion and were subjected to close and not always friendly surveillance if they elected even on what they thought were good medical grounds to give narcotics to an addict over anything other than a short period of time, and then in rapidly decreasing doses, or expressed an interest in research in narcotic drugs and narcotic addiction. Yet answers had to be found which could be applied in prevention and treatment of the condition.

It was true that addiction was recognized by many as a neglected medical problem of such importance that it could be dealt with adequately only at the federal level. At this time the Public Health Service was in the Treasury Department, as was the Narcotics Bureau, and it was felt that these two agencies in the same Department could work together productively to yield the needed answers. In 1928 a bill was introduced in Congress to authorize construction of two hospitals for the confinement and treatment of persons addicted to the use of habit-forming drugs. The bill was signed into law in 1929.

The first of these two hospitals for addicts was constructed at Lexington, Kentucky, and was originally known as the First U.S. Narcotic Farm. It was opened in 1935 with Dr. Lawrence Kolb, a psychiatrist who was a distinguished authority in the field of narcotic addiction, in charge. This hospital was so planned that it contained within it a research unit which consisted both of basic laboratory facilities and clinical beds in order that investigations of addiction could be carried out on a broad base. Doctor Kolb himself had conducted important research in this area at the Hygienic Laboratory of the Public Health service, the precursor of the National Institutes of Health, and his reports of his studies still remain classics in the field. The original staff at the Lexington Hospital consisted of basic and clinical investigators as well as clinicians recruited for the treatment of addiction. The Second U.S. Narcotic Farm was opened at Fort Worth, Texas, in 1938. The names of both of these hospitals were later changed to eliminate the words "narcotic farm." They are now known as U.S. Public Health Service Hospitals.

Under the act there was created within the Public Health Service a Narcotics Division to administer the hospitals and to carry out research on addiction and rehabilitation of addicts. Very soon after the research began it became apparent that although addiction itself is a physiological phenomenon its real etiological roots extend deeply into the personality of the victim. It was rare to find a true addict who did not present complex psychological and social problems which antedated his addiction. In studying these conditions and in advising the states with regard to programs for the control of addiction, it was inevitable that to a greater and greater extent the consultation centered about problems of mental health and mental disease. The Narcotics Division existed only a year as a formal entity, for in 1930 its scope was enlarged to include investigations related not only to drugs but to the causes, prevalence, and means for the prevention and treatment of mental and nervous diseases. The Federal Government was fully in the mental hygiene field for the first time, and the name of the Narcotics Division was changed to the Division of Mental Hygiene.

Now, finally, the civilian mental health activities of the government were, for the most part, centered in one agency. It was during the 1930s, under the direction of Dr. Walter L. Treadway, Chief of the new Division, that these activities were consolidated and an organized federal program begun. Now the government was involved with addicts in ways other than apprehension and punishment and/or detoxification. It was also involved with states and communities in cooperating to provide treatment and facilities for addicts; it was involved in studies of the cause, treatment, and prevention of mental illness —and it was involved in these things through a central agency.

Since the Federal Government was involved in the medical management and treatment of certain individuals, namely addicts, who had violated the law, usually as a result of their medical condition and were confined as a consequence thereof, it was logical that attention should be directed also to other classes of federal-law violators confined in the same penal system. The Federal Bureau of Prisons in the Department of Justice was headed by Mr. Sanford Bates, a courageous pioneer in the enlightened management and rehabilitation of the offender. It was inevitable that such a man would ask that this service be extended to other types of prisoners. As a result of this the Mental Hygiene Division of the Public Health Service was assigned the additional responsibility of the provision of medical and psychiatric services in federal prisons. This development has had a profound effect upon the philosophy behind the administration of the federal prisons, not only during Mr. Bates' administration but to an even greater degree under that of his successor, the distinguished James V. Bennett, who has for many years been a world leader in this field.

In 1936 Doctor Treadway was succeeded by Dr. Lawrence Kolb, the psychiatrist mentioned earlier who had contributed so much to the understanding of narcotic addiction. It was during Doctor Kolb's administration that the idea of a national neuropsychiatric institute came into being. He envisioned the institute as having both clinical and basic research facilities for the comprehensive study of mental and nervous diseases. He further advocated that the institute should be able to allocate funds to competent research groups throughout the country after appropriate review. There were many hurdles to overcome in bringing such a concept into reality. Precedent was on Kolb's side because the National Cancer Institute had been established in 1937. The draft plan was enthusiastically endorsed by the Section on Nervous and Mental Diseases of the American Medical Association, the American Psychiatric Association, the American Neurological Association, and the National Committee for Mental Hygiene. However, the time was not yet ripe for the great push forward. There were people in the country, including at least one influential professional organization, who questioned if this were a proper activity for the Federal Government or if an effort of this magnitude were justified in view of what was then known about the size of the problem. Kolb redrafted his proposal in the form of a bill to be introduced in Congress, but just as it looked as though there might be favorable results, World War II intervened and the bill was never introduced.

Thus World War II entered upon the scene, frustrating efforts to launch a program of research to better understand mental and emotional disorders but at the same time providing the data, some of which were cited at the beginning of this lecture, which constituted some of the convincing facts making up the justification for much broader legislation which was to be enacted a half decade later.

War, however deplorable it may be, has the paradoxical attribute of revealing facts and statistics and situations that otherwise might take decades to come to light. Here finally was the fertile ground, tilled tragically by unwanted struggle, watered with the blood of many nations, in which the dreams and the words of Clifford

Beers, the statesmanship and plan of Lawrence Kolb, and the many hopes of other Americans whom they had inspired would bloom and grow into reality.

In 1945 it appeared that the time was ripe for strong public action in the field of mental health. The data mentioned earlier were well documented and known by many informed people both in and out of Congress. There was serious concern about the implications for the future if positive action were not taken to better understand the causes and prevention of mental illnesses, to train adequately enough people to deal with the problems, and to assist the states in developing programs to combat mental and emotional disorders. Dr. Thomas Parran, then Surgeon General of the Public Health Service, was convinced of the need for a broad federal program in mental health. He gave strong encouragement and support to the development of legislation which would authorize a program that could deal effectively with the problems with which the country was faced.

The facts were also known to some of the leaders of Congress and they were in the mood for launching a new program to correct the situation. In 1945 Representative J. Percy Priest of Tennessee, in the House of Representatives, and Senators Claude Pepper of Florida, Lister Hill of Alabama, Robert A. Taft of Ohio, George Aiken of Vermont, Robert La Follette, Jr., of Wisconsin, and a number of others from both sides of the aisle in the Senate, introduced identical bills in the two houses, the stated purpose of which was "to improve the mental health of the people of the United States. . . ."

These bills—H.R. 2550 and S. 1160, 79th Congress—set forth three general purposes: fostering and aiding research relating to the cause, diagnosis, and treatment of neuropsychiatric disorders; providing for training of personnel through the award of fellowships to individuals and grants to public and non-profit institutions; and aid to the states, through grants and other assistance, in the formation and establishment of clinics and treatment centers, and the provision of pilot and demonstration programs in the prevention, diagnosis, and treatment of neuropsychiatric disorders. These bills went further than any previous health legislation in providing for training grants to institutions as well as training stipends and fellowships to individuals; they also contained the concept of direct assistance to the states—a type of support utilized in authorizing two previous health programs, those concerned with venereal disease and tuberculosis, but not written into other legislation which was more research-oriented, such as the act authorizing the National Cancer Institute.

To implement these goals and at the same time serve as a guardian of the public interest, the bill also provided for the creation of a National Advisory Mental Health Council. This council was charged with the responsibility of reviewing applications for research and training grants and the bill provided that no grant for assistance of research or training could be made unless the application were recommended favorably by the Advisory Council. The Council was also charged with advising the Surgeon General on all programs of the Public Health

Service where mental health matters were concerned. The members of this council were not to be government officials, except that there were to be two ex-officio members, one designated by the Secretary of Defense and the other by the Administrator of Veterans' Affairs. It should be said parenthetically here that probably no single provision of the legislation which proceeded from these bills has had a more significant effect upon the direction the mental health program has taken and upon its growth than has that establishing the National Advisory Mental Health Council. The quality of individuals selected to serve on this group, their dedication and sound advice from the very beginning, has involved both the professional and nonprofessional public and has brought their concerns and needs into the Institute's plans and operations.

Support for the bills came from all segments of society and there were few objections raised to their purpose or their need. Leaders of the neuropsychiatric programs of the Armed Services during the war, leaders in the mental health movement in the country at large, citizens concerned with the problems of children and adults, with delinquency, with mental health in the schools, and with many other mental health aspects of everyday living, appeared and placed their recommendations upon the record. It was pointed out that the proposed legislation did not violate the traditional separation of federal and state powers, but that the primary responsibility for operating and financing the programs would rest, as always, with the states and local communities to the limit of their resources and that federal assistance would be supplementary to local endeavor and not a substitution for it.

It would have taken a very different Congress than existed in 1945–1946 to withstand the massed weight of testimony which recommended support of the bills.[7] Not only were cogent data advanced to demonstrate the need for such legislation, but the witnesses from all walks of life stated their desire that the bill be enacted into law in order that they could expect a greater degree of mental health and a fuller life for themselves and their children.

In the course of hearings and committee action, some modifications were made in the original bills, but their fundamental objectives were not altered and their provisions which would allow a vigorous, forward thrust were not attenuated. The bills were enacted into law and signed by President Truman on July 3, 1946.

An interesting sidelight on the rapid-moving events of this time should be noted. The President signed the bill on July 3, 1946, and Congress adjourned the next day, July 4. The result of this was that there was a law on the books authorizing a vigorous program in mental health research, training, and service; but no funds were provided to implement the Act. It was felt essential that there be an early meeting of the National Advisory Mental Health Council which was promptly appointed as the law provided, but there were no funds to call a meeting of the Body, once created. Those responsible for getting the program underway then did what program directors and scientific investigators have done before and since. The rounds of the private foundations were made in an effort to obtain sufficient assistance at least to call a meeting of the Advisory Council. In New York City the Greentree Foundation (no longer in existence) listened sympathetically to the needs for funds and awarded a grant of fifteen thousand dollars for this purpose. It has always seemed particularly significant that the National Institute of Mental Health which awarded funds to so many grantees for training and research purposes and to assist the states, had its origin in a grant made by private philanthropy. Throughout the years of the growth and development of the Institute, this fact was never lost sight of by the staff, and those who had need of support, while not always receiving it for many reasons, at least always received a sympathetic hearing and often a great deal more empathic reaction on the part of the Institute personnel than the applicant ever dreamed.

The Council met, basic policies were laid down, plans were formulated, and the program was underway. In 1947, when the Congress returned to Washington, it enacted the first appropriation and the Federal Government's participation in a National Mental Health Program unmatched in the history of the world, either in size or in scope, was launched.

Throughout the remainder of the decade of the forties the arousal of the American people was rapid and dramatic. Much of the stigma of mental illness, which had been prevalent since time immemorial, began to fall away. Mental and emotional disorders were spoken of much more frankly and the need for increased knowledge, more skilled manpower, and facilities of all types was increasingly accepted.

By the close of the decade the states and communities were moving forward energetically on a number of fronts. There was a marked increase in research in universities and other laboratories throughout the country, and these studies covered a wide range of problems relevant to neurology and psychiatry. A review of reports from those days reveals the appearance of the names of distinguished investigators who had formerly not worked in the field, as well as those of young men and women who had become interested in the problems of nervous and mental disorders. Research was being carried on in such areas as neuroanatomy, neurophysiology, the biochemistry of behavior, neurological conditions, emotional development of children, multiple sclerosis, epilepsy, psychosomatic disorders, etiology, treatment of schizophrenia, genetics, and the role of the family in personality development, to name a few. Training of additional professionals to work in the mental health field was going forward rapidly. The original training efforts were directed toward the preparation of teachers who could help to fill the needs for staff in departments of psychology, psychiatry, social work, and psychiatric nursing throughout the country. A number of new training programs were initiated and existing programs were expanded. One of the most significant developments insofar as its impact upon training programs was concerned was a program of grants awarded to educators in the mental health disciplines to explore methods and procedures for improving the quality of training in their program.

In the area of mental health services, whereas at the time of passage of the act only twenty states had mental health programs of any type other than the care of patients in public hospitals, inadequate as that was in many cases, now all but three states had a mental health program and some were well developed. The number of mental health clinics in the states had increased from slightly over 800 to over 1,200, of which three-quarters were supported locally and without federal assistance. The care and treatment of patients in hospitals also had improved. Staffing ratios were better and those persons caring for patients were better prepared. The decline in hospital populations which has been so dramatic in recent years had not yet begun, however, and the fact that the number of patients continued to increase was a matter of considerable concern. Voluntary groups dedicated to improving the mental health picture increased in number and in activity and were having their effect upon the actions of legislatures to improve the plight of the hospitalized mentally ill as well as those in extramural settings.

All of these things being done were good, of course, but they were merely the foundation upon which would be built the amazing developments yet to come. It was generally accepted that there must be some radical new development before a real breakthrough could occur.

These events were standing in the wings waiting for their cue, and would enter on stage in the decade to come.

Thus the first half of the twentieth century drew to a close. The mental hygiene movement had appeared, flourished, and grown. The Nation recognized its responsibility for the mentally ill after having been faced with the alarming statistics which grew out of the world-wide holocaust known as World War II. The Federal Government accepted its responsibility and its role, and legislation was passed. States and communities moved promptly to do their part; the professions grasped the opportunity better to serve those to whom they were dedicated; the first small trickle of new knowledge, which would later become a flood, was coming from the laboratories.

In retrospect, it looks as though the great developments should have been apparent to everyone. On the contrary, many were concerned for fear the forward momentum which the mental health movement had acquired would wane and high hopes would be dashed. This was not to be. There had been a change in philosophy with regard to the mentally ill, a change in thinking as to how to attack the problem, and a change in the attitude of the public toward these conditions. Few people realized it, but the revolution had begun.

CHAPTER III

THE OPENING DOOR

ONE NOT INFREQUENTLY finds difficulty in differentiating between revolution and evolution. If change takes place over a short period of time it may be explosive in character and spoken of as a revolution. The concept of revolution usually carries with it a threat of violent action, even if no violence actually occurs. Evolution on the other hand is usually thought of as the process of mutation—of step by step change from one form or state to another.

At the close of my last lecture I stated that the revolution in the field of mental health and mental illness had begun. I used that word advisedly. The changes were rapid during the 1950s, sometimes explosive in character. As the concept of comprehensive mental health programs began to spread across the length and breadth of the land, it was not always met with rejoicing and enthusiastic acceptance. Many overburdened administrators of programs felt they were extended beyond the limit of their ability and could not take on and properly administer another new activity. Yet the public demand grew and the pressure increased for the inauguration or expansion, without delay, of mental health services of all types.

The advance of mental health programs in the United States, ranging from the reform movement begun by Clifford Beers early in this century through the National Committee for Mental Hygiene to the effort to return care and treatment of the mentally ill to the community in which they live, is to be understood only through insight into the character of the American people, for this was a program of and for the people. There are aspects of the culture in this land which are a reflection, if not a lineal descendant, of the pioneers who won the wilderness and developed the country. Many of the distinctive features of our society, and indeed its paradoxes, develop from this frontier spirit. As a nation we emphasize technology and the affluent society and all they make possible in terms of luxury and comfort, but at the same time we also stress the importance of education for its own sake—for the esthetic enriching of our lives.

It has been said that as a people we are aggressive and individualistic—qualities which foster flexibility in our thinking and a capacity to make changes. We have an optimistic conviction that what we feel should be done should be attempted now, without too much regard for tradition or precedent, and that our efforts will triumph. This national characteristic is typical of nearly all our efforts; the attitude that denies the impossible, the refusal to give up the search or the endeavor although the evidence often does not indicate easy success.

In so many of our advances into new fields we have followed this bent of our pioneer spirit, convinced that frontiers exist only to be pushed back. We boast of our exploits: we are Paul Bunyan, Johnny Appleseed, and Pecos Bill, blended into one—asserting our dominion over the frontiers with goodhearted and joyful power, with a feeling for our fellows and their welfare, and with an enthusiasm almost completely untamed.

The physical frontier was our prisoner long before we realized the importance of the social frontier. As we have seen, our advances in areas of social need, in self-preservation, in tempering exuberance with understanding, came at times when we were forced to use the process of self-examination.

We are probably the most self-critical people in the world, but we do not engage in self-examination as a national pastime. When, however, sufficiently convincing data are presented to alert those in the local and national power structure that all is not well in some phase of our life, the wheels are set in motion and we embark upon the task. Once we know the dimensions of the problem and its importance, there is a demand for the remedies to be forthcoming. The response of the people is often awesome in its size and lusty enthusiasm.

The National Mental Health Act of 1946, enacted into law at the insistence of an informed and aroused America, was this kind of response. However, despite the social and medical significance of the Act in terms of the long step it took us forward toward utilizing our resources with maximum effort in dealing with the problems of mental illnesses, it was something of a step out of step. What we had done with the Act was to prescribe for the symptoms before we had the diagnosis, knowing full well that a more searching diagnostic study would have to be made, and made in the near future.

There had been forward movements since the passage of the Act. The appropriations to the National Institute of Mental Health had increased from 8,700,000 dollars in 1950 as the decade opened, to 18 million dollars in 1956, and it was obvious they would increase much more. Parenthetically, this figure more than trebled to 68 million dollars in fiscal year 1960 which began in the last half of 1959, and for which the funds were voted in the last year of the decade of the fifties. These funds made possible a greatly increased amount of research and training throughout the country, as well as significantly increased programs of service. There began in 1956 the longed-for decrease in the number of patients in public mental hospitals, which continued without interruption throughout the rest of the decade; and in fact, until the present time. The number of physicians working in public mental hospitals had increased, but staff in this category was still only slightly over 50 per cent of adequacy. The number of psychiatrists in the United States in all types of practice showed a 57 per cent increase from 5,534 in 1950 to 8,713 in 1956, and during the remainder of the decade showed a further increase of 35 per cent to over 12,000. According to Albee [1] there were about 7,000 members of the American Psychological Association in 1950, which rose to 14,700 in 1956, and to over 19,000 in 1961. A significant number of these new psychologists and psychiatrists were in their fields as a result of the program which the Congress had assigned to the

National Institute of Mental Health. The number of social workers and nurses had also increased significantly, social workers by 25 per cent and nurses by 150 per cent, but the exact number who were available to mental health programs is difficult to determine. There were large and energetic training programs for members of these disciplines in the field of mental health, and it is known that departments enlarged and the enrollments increased significantly as a result of these efforts. New knowledge was being accumulated at an ever-increasing rate. The psychoactive drugs were beginning to be used by 1956 and were to have a definite impact on the size of mental hospital populations by 1960. New techniques of treatment and management of patients were developing, but prompt communication of scientific knowledge was still a problem to be solved.

There had been gratifying advances in all areas of endeavor, and results were being produced. Still, to an impatient nation the advances were not far enough, fast enough, or on a broad enough conceptual base.

As a result, in 1955 a Joint Resolution [2] was passed without a dissenting vote by a Congress that recognized the time had come for an appraisal of our situation. The Mental Health Study Act of 1955, signed into law by President Eisenhower on July 28 of that year, authorized an appropriation to be awarded by the National Institute of Mental Health as a grant to study and make recommendations regarding the various facets of mental health and mental illness in the United States.

The Resolution spelled out some of the known facts concerning the problem, and did so in lucid terms. It is a landmark document, describing as it does the situation in 1955:

Some 750,000 mentally ill and retarded patients were in hospitals on any given day, and 47 per cent of the hospital beds in the Nation were occupied by mental patients.

The direct economic cost of mental illnesses to the taxpayers of the Nation, including pensions to veterans with psychiatric disabilities, was over one billion dollars a year and had been increasing at a rate of one million dollars a year.

The emotional impact and distress suffered by millions of Americans anxiously and justifiably concerned about the welfare, treatment, and prospects of mentally afflicted relatives was incalculable and was one of the most urgent concerns of our people.

The Governors of the several states, through national and regional Governors' Conferences and through the publications of the Council of State Governments, had shown great initiative in their cooperative attempts to develop better methods of meeting the challenge of mental illnesses in their states.

There was strong justification for believing that this constantly growing burden may well have been due primarily to an outmoded reliance on simple custodial care in mental hospitals as the chief method of dealing with mental illnesses.

There was strong reason to believe that lack of early intensive treatment facilities had created such a backlog of mentally deteriorated patients that it had become virtually impossible for the states to meet the need for mental hospital facilities.

There seemed to be a discouraging lag between the discovery of new knowledge and skills in treating mental illness and their widespread application, as was evidenced by the fact that whereas only about one-third of newly admitted mental patients were discharged in the course of a year, in a few outstanding institutions the discharge rate was 75 per cent or more.

Experience with certain community outpatient clinics and rehabilitation centers began to give indication that many mental patients could be better treated on an outpatient basis at much lower cost than by a hospital.

There was strong reason to believe that a substantial proportion of public mental hospital facilities were being utilized for the care of elderly persons who could be better cared for and receive better treatment at lower cost in modified facilities.

There was reason to believe that many emotionally disturbed children were being placed in mental hospitals which had no proper facilities to minister to their needs.

Mental illnesses were frequently a component of such nationwide problems as alcoholism, drug addiction, juvenile delinquency, broken homes, school failures, absenteeism, job maladjustments in industry, and suicide.

Finally, there seemed to be no over-all integrated body of knowledge concerning all aspects of the present status of our resources, methods, and practices for diagnosing, treating, caring for, and rehabilitating the mentally ill, although only through the development of such a body of knowledge could the people of the United States ascertain the true nature of this staggering problem and develop more effective plans to meet it.

Those, then, were the items that comprised the bill of particulars. They touched on the situation as it was at that time, the needs that were so immediate, and the encouraging aspects that did exist. The Resolution went on:

It is the sense of the Congress that there exists a critical need for such an objective, thorough, and nationwide analysis and re-evaluation of the human and economic problems of mental illness and of the resources, methods, and practices currently utilized in diagnosing, treating, caring for, and rehabilitating the mentally ill, both within and outside of institutions, as may lead to the development of comprehensive and realistic recommendations for such better utilization of those resources or such improvements on and new developments in methods of diagnosis, treatment, care, and rehabilitation as giving promise of resulting in a marked reduction in the incidence or duration of mental illness, and, in consequence, a lessening of the appalling emotional and financial drain on the families of those afflicted or on the economic resources of the States and of the Nation.

It is declared to be the policy of the Congress to promote mental health and to help solve the complex and the interrelated problems posed by mental illness by encouraging the undertaking of nongovernmental, multidisciplinary research into and reevaluation of all aspects of our resources, methods, and practices for diagnosing, treating, caring for, and rehabilitating the mentally ill, including research aimed at the prevention of mental illness. It is the purpose of this Joint Resolution to implement that policy.

This implementation took the form of an authorization for the appropriation of funds in amounts not to exceed 250,000 dollars for the first year and 500,000 dollars for each of the next two, which were to be expended as grants to be made through the National Institute of Mental Health, upon the recommendation of the National Advisory Mental Health Council, to an organization or organizations for a program of research into and studies of resources and needs. Such organization or organizations were to seek other funds also, hopefully in at least an equal amount, in order that the study could be extended and complete. Upon completion of the study and research a report was to be made to the Congress, the Executive Branch of the Government, and the people generally through the governors of their states. The establishment of the Joint Commission on Mental Illness and Health, an organization made up of representatives of thirty-six participating agencies, had been effected earlier in 1955 and, following approval of their application, the mandate of the Congress devolved upon them. The members of this Body felt that on the basis of the situation as they found it their studies and reports should center around three principal problems, namely: manpower, facilities, and costs of care of the mentally ill. They conceived of their purpose as determining the facts insofar as they were able to do so, in order to prepare a final report which would recommend a national program that would approach adequacy in meeting the individual needs of the mentally ill, and to develop a plan of action which would ensure the authorities, both professional and governmental, that the plan was adequate to meet the needs.

The Commission was made up of a diverse group of professionals and volunteers who had in common concern about mental health and mental illnesses. Physicians were represented through several organizations, among which were the American Medical Association, the American Psychiatric Association, and the American Academy of Pediatrics. Also represented were public health workers, psychologists, biologists, sociologists, nurses, occupational therapists, welfare experts, mental health educators, clergymen, and many citizens' organizations, including such groups as the American Legion, the National Association for Mental Health, and the Council of State Governments.

The Joint Commission went to work on its task in 1956, following an appropriation by the Congress of the first year's funds in the authorized amount of 250,000 dollars. The studies and investigations were carried out by outstanding authorities and scholars from numerous fields who utilized widely accepted methodological procedures. They were divided into ten task forces, each dealing with one of the following areas: (1) Current concepts of positive mental health; (2) Economics of mental illness; (3) Mental health manpower trends; (4) Americans view their mental health; (5) Community resources and mental health; (6) Epidemiology of mental illness; (7) The role of schools in mental health; (8) The churches and mental health; (9) New prospectives of mental patient care; and (10) Research resources in mental health. The findings of these studies, which were completed in 1960, provided the basis for the major recommendations presented in the volume *Action for Mental Health*,[3] published in 1961, which was the official report of the Commission as required by the Act. The findings and recommendations were set forth in a clear and cogent manner that focused national attention upon the broad spectrum of problems related to mental health and mental illnesses in this country. The persistent problem areas in the field—those of manpower, facilities, and costs—were clearly identified, their dimensions projected. Thoughtful and in many instances provocative approaches to their solution were proposed.

The major thesis of the Commission, as stated in the report, was that "It is impossible to separate the patients who must be cared for from the persons who must be trained to care for them; and it is impossible to separate either patients or professional personnel from the search for new knowledge of vital concern to both." In this context a major observation of the Commission was that in terms of today's and future needs there are insufficient personnel to provide either the services to the public, the research to find the answers, or the teaching staff to produce an adequate number of trained workers. These shortages, it was predicted, would be intensified if, in some manner, the manpower pool were not sufficiently increased or new patterns of utilization found over the decade ahead.

Another of the Commission's significant observations was that the demand for treatment would increase as facilities become more widely and more readily available. The Commission anticipated, therefore, that the ranks of the untreated mentally ill who seek treatment will grow even faster than the demand indicated on the basis of population growth alone. It concluded that the severely mentally ill are "the unfinished business" in the mental health field.

The Commission, asserting that science and education are resources to be conserved, stressed the need for basic research "to specify the causes and characteristics sufficiently so that we can predict and therefore prevent various forms of mental illness or disordered behavior. . . ." It called for long-term research, support for investigators, and establishment of mental health research centers.

Emphasis was placed on the need for broad policies of assistance to the mentally ill by all groups of those with mental health knowledge and aptitudes—professional or not; it called for expanded programs of mental health training; it advocated wider programs of general as well as medical and scientific education.

Services, it maintained, should be made available to emotionally disturbed children through the increased use of mental health counselors, mental health consultants, pediatricians, and new types of resident schools for children.

Emergency psychiatric care must be available within the sick person's community, and intensive care must be available through such community resources as mental health clinics, general hospitals, and mental hospitals. The Commission recommended smaller mental hospitals of 1,000 beds or less as intensive treatment centers, and said that an adequate portion of existing mental hospitals should be converted into facilities for the care of chronic mental patients.

Aftercare and rehabilitation services were regarded as essential to enable the patient to maintain himself in his community following hospitalization.

Finally, the Commission looked at costs and said, "Expenditures for public mental patient services should be doubled in the next five years—and tripled in the next ten." It called for increased participation by the Federal Government in financing services, since states and communities could not afford the cost necessary to bring care of the mentally ill onto a par with care of the physically ill.

The report was heavily weighted on the side of inpatient care of the mentally ill—a conscious choice of the Commission. A criticism of a number of people, including those who were then in charge of the National Institute of Mental Health, was that considerably more attention could have been placed upon steps aimed at prevention of mental illnesses and upon maintenance of mental health in the development of a "National Action" program. The Commission observed that its principles for federal, state, and local matching grants did not attempt to compensate for the varying needs and resources of the states as measured by such criteria as population, patient load, relative levels of expenditures, and per capita income. As a footnote it is difficult to see how the proposal could have been adequately developed without major consideration being given to these among other variables.

This whole problem of patient population as it relates to public mental hospitals, with all it connotes in terms of treatment procedures, staffing patterns, employee morale, and the like, had been a matter of concern to those working in the mental health field for many years. Somehow it did not seem that hospitalization in large institutions, sometimes far removed from the homes of the patients, was a logical procedure. If one were to relate all procedures and treatments to the etiology of illness it seemed as though more attention should be given to keeping the patient in his home community. This concept centered on the fact that people who become mentally ill usually become so in their homes, among their family members, in their own neighborhoods. Their illness is not an isolated occurrence, dependent upon nothing around them. If they become ill in the community, if the community is in truth a contributing factor in their illness, then it must follow that true recovery, or even recovery to such an extent that they can function effectively, hinges upon adjustment to and in the community. By community is meant home, work, and neighborhood. This belief encompasses a number of medical and psychiatric concepts—including a public health approach to the problem, the primary idea of which is prevention.

Whether one is talking of mental illnesses, typhoid fever, or tuberculosis, the fundamental concept is the same: the community can be nurturing and helpful or it can be toxic and hostile. In any event, if one is to recover from one's illness, whatever type it may be, one must return home eventually. Not to do so is, in effect, not to have fully recovered. The concept of the community goes deeper than this, however, for, as with typhoid fever or tuberculosis, there can exist foci of infection which, when the circumstances are right and the patient's resistance is low, may be the producer of an illness which can incapacitate or overwhelm one. Thus, as one thinks of the rehabilitation of the individual who is already sick one turns immediately to consideration of the factors in the community which will be supportive of the person or which will tend to be destructive. In mental illnesses and mental health, as with tuberculosis, these considerations encompass many aspects of the community. One is concerned with such problems as housing, unemployment, prejudice, and other sources of social and psychological tension in the neighborhood as well as in the home. If one is to carry this concept to its logical conclusion, one would say that a community can be therapeutic or destructive, depending upon a variety of elements. By therapeutic is meant supportive and helpful in all aspects, not merely through the organized agencies whose responsibility is caretaking. When these factors exist in a community and there is added the element of skilled personnel to care for those who need professional help, the community contains within itself the elements necessary to maintain or restore health, mental or physical. By the same token, as one considers those who are not yet overtly ill but who are vulnerable, the same elements in the community are important. Appropriate facilities for emotional support, when needed, and for advice and counseling, when indicated, can spell the difference between continued health and mental illness. Finally, the positive aspects of mental health must be given attention. Within the community should lie those factors for character building and for positive mental health which contribute to a more rugged and resilient state of mental health. This means much more than merely fending off mental illness. Advice, consultation, and a focal point for some of the action programs are usually needed.

Thus was born the concept of the comprehensive community mental health center which was so strongly hinted at in the Joint Commission report. The feasibility of a comprehensive community center was based on a number of foundation stones, without which it would have been impossible to develop the idea to the working stage. These included improvements in state mental hospitals that allowed treatment of patients in extramural settings; the advent of the psycho-active drugs; the reversal of the alarming growth of mental hospital populations; the increase in treatment of psychiatric ills in general hospitals; and the growth of the trained mental health manpower pool.[4]

During the years that the Joint Commission was carrying out its task an important change took place in Washington. A president entered the White House who had a long-standing concern for the mentally ill and retarded, and who combined with this a determination to do something about the then existing situation. It was to this President that the Joint Commission submitted its final report, "Action for Mental Health," in 1961.

President Kennedy appointed a Cabinet-level committee to analyze the report and to recommend legislative action to be taken in implementing it. This committee consisted of the Secretary of the Department of Health, Education, and Welfare, as Chairman; the Secretary of Labor; and the Administrator of Veterans' Affairs. As advisers to this committee the President called upon the Bureau of the Budget and the Council of Economic Advisors. The committee was directed to consider the Joint Commission report in all of its aspects, and to make recommendations to the President which would consist of an action program consistent with the policies of the Government which the President could propose to the Congress. The report and recommendations of the committee were submitted to the President and accepted by him. His acceptance of these recommendations was followed by the formulation of an eloquent message from him to the Congress on February 5, 1963.[5] That historic document was the first ever promulgated by the head of any government devoted exclusively to mental illness and mental retardation and stating his government's position in favor of doing all possible for these handicapped citizens. The words of the message had such a sense of urgency that neither the Congress nor the American people could ignore them. Every American was involved, for, as President Kennedy said, "governments at every level—federal, state, and local—private foundations, and individual citizens must all face up to their responsibilities." Then he enumerated the responsibilities, echoing the words of the Study Act of 1955 and the final report of the Joint Commission.

"First," he said, "we must seek out the causes of mental illness and mental retardation and eradicate them." The hope implied in this statement was based on the progress made during the past two decades, especially progress which far exceeded any of the hopes and expectations expressed two decades before. It also implied that Americans found it difficult to believe that so little had been done about such an important national health problem during the first half of this century.

But because of the recent advances—and President Kennedy spoke of many that we have discussed here—he felt that we could increasingly turn to the prevention of mental disabilities which he described as far more economical and far more likely to be successful than custodial care. To this end he envisioned the expansion of training programs as probably the most important aspect of the battle against mental illness.

"We must strengthen the underlying resources of knowledge and, above all, of skilled manpower." He felt that we could take pride in the fact that professional manpower had increased significantly, in some categories two or more fold; but he looked farther than the present, and said that while we had increased the number of trained professional persons available to work in the mental health field, we should be thinking in terms of doubling all mental health manpower in a decade: from 45,000 in 1960 to more than 85,000 in 1970.

Finally, he stressed the importance of coordinated action. In his words, "we must strengthen and improve the programs and facilities serving the mentally ill and the mentally retarded." Here he proposed a network of comprehensive community mental health centers covering the United States to allow for treatment of the patient near his home, in the community where he lives. A variety of successful treatment programs were at that time in operation across the country, and they were operating successfully in community facilities. He proposed that these services, where they existed in a community, be assembled into a comprehensive treatment entity, and that similar services be available in many more communities.

In addition to recommending federal funds for assistance on a declining basis to help staff the centers, and to make sure that they effectively filled the community's needs, he recommended a program of planning grants to the states for a period of two years during which they would survey their needs and resources and formulate a comprehensive mental health program which would fill the needs of all their citizens.

Speaking of the day when the approach embodied in the recommendations would be an accomplished fact, President Kennedy said, "reliance on the cold mercy of custodial isolation will be supplanted by the open warmth of community concern and capability. Emphasis on prevention, treatment, and rehabilitation will be substituted for a desultory interest in confining patients in an institution to wither away."

President Kennedy summed up his recommended approach in these words:

> I am convinced that, if we apply our medical knowledge and social insights fully, all but a small portion of the mentally ill can eventually achieve a wholesome and constructive adjustment. . . .
>
> If we launch a broad new mental health program now, it will be possible within a decade or two to reduce the number of patients now under custodial care by 50 per cent or more. Many more mentally ill can be helped to remain in their own homes without hardship to themselves or their families. Those who are hospitalized can be helped to return to their own communities. All but a small proportion can be restored to useful life. We can spare them and their families much of the misery which mental illness now entails. We can save public funds and we can conserve our manpower resources.

The result was first an appropriation by the Congress of 4.2 million dollars for matching grants to the states to plan for their mental health needs. This process was supported for another year in the same amount and the two-year final reports, in addition to serving as guidelines for the states—the states agreed to exchange information regarding their plans, so all could profit thereby—were studied and utilized at the National Institute of Mental Health for purposes of planning the program on a national level. In addition, funds were appropriated for grants to mental hospitals for improvement of discreet treatment projects. These grants were designed to serve as examples in the hospital and its region of what could and should be done in mental hospitals to better treat and care for the hospitalized mentally ill. Grants were also made to provide inservice training experience for mental hospital aides and other nonprofessional personnel in order that they could more intelligently and effectively carry out the prescribed procedures of psychiatrists and other professionals designed to bring the patient back to mental health and ultimately return him to his home community.

But the most important activity during that summer of 1963 was the introduction of bills to provide 150 million dollars in mental health center construction grants and nearly 500 million dollars in center staffing funds. Hearings before Congressional committees convinced the Congress of the need for construction assistance, but the climate was such that they abandoned the idea of providing the essential staffing assistance. It was not that this was thought to be unnecessary, but rather the pressure from powerful groups was such that political tacticians felt it was advisable to drop this proposed authorization. As a result the subcommittee and then the full committee of the House of Representatives failed to report out the essential staffing provision.

The construction bill [6] finally passed in the early autumn of 1963 and it was signed by President Kennedy on October 30, approximately three weeks before his death.

During the months intervening between passage of that bill and the opening of the first session of the 89th Congress it became evident that many communities needed services as much as, or even more than, new buildings. It is difficult to move quickly into new programs without financial help from some source, and community after community expressed the critical need for interim assistance until a new structure of support at the local level could be achieved. In response, the Congress in 1965 enacted the essential legislation [7] which had been abandoned before and which provided a total of 224,750,000 dollars for short-term staffing assistance. This assistance would be available to a center on application and adequate justification, on a declining basis, for the center's first fifty-one months of operation.

These two pieces of legislation taken together are introducing in the United States a new era of community-centered comprehensive mental health care and services.

This new era—during which it is expected that about 500 community mental health centers will be built by 1970—holds the promise of ending forever the neglect and isolation which has been the lot of the mentally ill, both in and out of hospitals, since the dawn of time.

It holds the promise of returning the practice of psychiatry to the mainstream of American medicine.

It holds the promise of extending into many realms of our everyday life the productive use of the new insights into man's nature which the biological and behavioral sciences have developed in the twentieth century.

It holds the promise that in our generation we can lighten immeasurably, and for all time, the great burden the mental illnesses have in the past placed upon mankind.

But—great as this promise is, it will be lost unless the

momentum which has been developed is continued and accelerated. The most must be made, both of the promise and the opportunities we now have, or we shall lose them, and the effort must be made soon, or much of our accomplishments in the political field will be for naught.

The new programs we have are, first and foremost, programs of the people and for the people. They must be carried out by the people. Each community and state must push forward to see that the mental health needs of all the people will be met.

We cannot, however, enter into this effort blithely and blindly. If we are to see our efforts crowned with success, so that the mentally ill can be well served, our lives will, of necessity, become more crowded and complicated. All that has been demanded of us in the past will be little compared with the demands of the next few years.

Unfortunately, the old system of care is deeply woven into the tapestry of our time. It lives in buildings, in the minds of men, in our statute books. It is reinforced each day by the subtle and not-so-subtle actions of hundreds and thousands of men and women. And somehow the tapestry must be rewoven.

The problems ahead involved with implementing the new concepts are difficult. For example, before a community mental health center is established it will be necessary for the community to know its present characteristics and what direction it is now taking or will be taking during the next several years. It will need to understand the problems its people are now facing and the problems they will be facing in the future.

These factors must be reviewed, and, in the light of the total social and psychological needs of people, as they now live and will be living, plans must be formulated for a mental health program that will respond to the needs of all the people in the community and still be economically feasible. Furthermore, as a center and its program are developing its effectiveness must be continually evaluated. This kind of research is rooted in the community itself, involves all the groups and forces in the community, and takes into account the needs, goals, and aspirations of the community. It takes into account, for example, the community's efforts to prevent mental illnesses, from the standpoint of public and community health in many ways the most important element of all.

The concept of preventive activities implies the extension of professional efforts and skills to the primary point in the cycle of health or social disability—that is, to the point before disability develops. It means making available to all elements in the population services which traditionally have been established to serve only the more vulnerable. Present knowledge and skills can be used to reinforce the healthy development that is crucial to good mental health by concentrating on critical periods or transition points in the life of the individual. Such events as entering school, adolescence, marriage, birth of children, retirement, and old age are convenient points of attack for a program of preventive intervention.

Next, it must be kept in mind that under the new program there will be no support for facilities or services that unnecessarily duplicate those already existing in a community. It will be essential to develop techniques for utilizing present resources and coordinating new developments with what is already available. If the community mental health center is to be effective it will have to provide a wide variety of services, but there may be difficulties in developing all of these resources within a short period.

It will be necessary, therefore, to cope with the problem of developing these services over an abbreviated span of time in such a way that the lack of total program does not negate the value of the newly developed activities. A tremendous amount of administrative resourcefulness and community cooperation must be developed. It will be necessary to gain cooperation not only from the medical resources of the community but from the social agencies, educational institutions, enforcement agencies, churches, and a wide variety of community groups if these new developments are to be effective.

In addition to the development of administrative resourcefulness and a consensus within the community of how the community programs should be developed there is a need to know a great deal more about the epidemiology of the mental illnesses, about the distribution of services and facilities of all types, and about how effective services and facilities are with various types of patients. Data must be collected from treatment resources in the community to reveal more about the characteristics of their patients—and this information must be properly analyzed, cross-checked, coordinated, and reported.

With regard to such a new program, there are few

issues that will be more important than knowing the number of trained professionals to work in the field of mental health and how their skills are to be used. There are not now, nor will there be in the foreseeable future, enough psychiatrists to enable them to be the sole medical practitioners dealing with the psychiatric illnesses. Thus if the treatment of the medical aspects of mental illnesses are to be in the hands of those medically trained, the non-psychiatric physician must become competent to deal with many of the psychiatric problems of his patients. In the realignment of professional roles among physicians this will inevitably follow the development of greater competence among all physicians in dealing with psychiatric problems. The role of the psychiatrist will increasingly become one demanding a high degree of skill as specialist-leader and as a specialized consultant.

At the same time there is a need to explore and evaluate aspects of the mental health problem present in the community which can be handled by other trained professionals; and there is need to know who these professionals are and what special training in mental health concepts and skills they require to deal effectively with the mental health problems they encounter as they fulfill their primary roles as clergymen, lawyers, teachers, youth leaders, probation officers, and others.

The problems are many and immense but they are not insurmountable. We have come a great distance, even from the fairly recent days of World War II. The care and treatment of mental illness are being returned to the community through the new national mental health program authorized by recent legislation. The doors of the mental hospitals are opening.

This discussion has focused primarily upon the legislative actions that led us to our present position. How these actions could be implemented, what the operational guidelines for the new community centers should be, is another story, intimately tied up with new modes of treatment, the use of psychoactive drugs, enlightened research, and new understandings.

All of these together play an important part in any consideration of the promise of the future in mental health, for the future is built on the past todays; and from what we have and are today we can envision what the future will be.

What is this promise of the future? Where can we expect to be in a decade, in two decades, as far as conquering the scourge of mental illness is concerned? How can we strengthen our resources for preserving and promoting mental health? What can we expect to know in the future which we do not now know? We will look at all of this in our final lecture.

CHAPTER IV

TOMORROW'S PROMISE

INSCRIBED above the National Archives Building in Washington, D.C., are the words, "The past is prologue." The story is told of a Washington cab driver, one of that amazing breed of political sages, curbstone consultants, and practical historians who make up the Washington Cabby Corps, who, while driving a fare past the building, asked if the passenger knew the meaning of the words carved in the marble. Without waiting for an answer the cabby said, "What that says in everyday English is, 'You ain't seen nothin' yet.' "

That is, I am certain, the situation where the conquest of mental illnesses is concerned; for, over the past two decades, professionals and general public alike have been moving with increasing enthusiasm and speed toward more rational and practical concepts of mental illnesses and methods, not only for overcoming but for preventing them.

It is within the lifetimes of many of us present here that the commonly accepted attitudes of today will have been rejected as unrealistic and impractical.

The memories of many physicians of my vintage of their first experiences with the hospitalized mentally ill are still vivid. The interest of many of them strayed from psychiatry when they realized that even the most fully qualified practitioner of that day did not possess sufficient knowledge, nor have at his disposal adequate social and medical resources to enable him to restore to mental health many of his patients. When one of us did choose psychiatry for his life's work he did so in spite of this, looking with envy on the successes of his colleagues in other fields of medicine. How he longed for similar advances and equally effective tools in order that he could bring more help and hope to those he served!

A vignette from my own past is typical. I well remember the reaction of my physician-father to my decision to become a psychiatrist. A general practitioner in a midwestern town, he had hopes that I would go more deeply into some branch of "real" medicine, as he called it, and hopefully would return home and enter practice with him. A psychiatrist was not his ideal of a physician, to put it mildly. The practice of psychiatry, he felt, had little to do with the practice of medicine, and the majority of those who practiced it did so because they either could not, or did not, choose to practice "scientific" medicine. I often wish he were alive today to see where psychiatry has gone as a branch of "real" medicine. I am certain, though, that in that heaven for overworked general practitioners he knows of the developments of the past two decades which have made psychiatry not only a part of medicine but have placed it at the very heart of it.

However, the attitude of my father reflected the thinking of the majority of his peers. Psychiatrists thirty-five or so years ago had less precise scientific knowledge and a smaller and less effective supply of specific therapies at their disposal. As a result, many of their patients, in spite of the psychiatrist's best efforts, became chronic psychiatric invalids who were doomed to live out their lives in institutions.

Along with these facts was a prevailing opinion—shared by many physicians with their nonmedical contemporaries—that the mentally ill were different from the physically ill, and in fact could return to full health and activity if they would "think positive thoughts," "get hold of themselves," and "straighten up and fly right." This negative attitude concerning mental illnesses also pervaded the thinking of the public generally, and it is that attitude which so long stood in the way of better understanding and acceptance of mental illnesses.

Yet, those physicians of the 1920s and 1930s laid the groundwork for the birth of the concept of community psychiatry. In their day the art of medicine was at least as important as its science. Understanding the patient as a person was essential. The art of observation was still the greatest attribute of the physician, and when a physician practiced this art he observed the whole man—the psychological and social as well as the physical. By that is meant that he observed the whole man in the context of his whole environment. The family doctor knew his families in detail; he knew the particulars as well as the generalities of the background and present condition of each member. Those physicians were remarkably successful in using their own medical wisdom and their knowledge of people which came with practice through the years to deal with the emotional problems of the patients they encountered in their day-to-day activities. Theirs was an age that lacked much of what we rather smugly today call "our sophistication" where mental illnesses are concerned; an age with fewer diagnostic centers and community hospitals; an age that predated many of today's specialized resources. Because the family physician was often not only his community's sole medical resource but was held by his neighbors to be one of their "wise men," he functioned in many capacities, dealing not only with the usual ills of the body, but with the emotional problems of his patients as well. He was called upon for advice and information in many areas. He was, of necessity, resourceful and intuitive. He used his medical skills, his knowledge of people and how they tolerated trouble, and he used, in addition, his influence as family counselor and friend. Truly he treated his patients for both physical and emotional ills.

Here was the precursor of our present-day concept of how to deal with the problem of mental illness and health. The community was concerned about and cared for its own. The family physician was the first contact point of his families when they needed medical care or advice. He dealt both with physical and mental ills. Emotional and mental problems constituted a significant part of his practice for it has been estimated on a national basis that at least one-third of the patients who make their way to the offices of physicians are suffering solely, or principally, from emotional problems, while another one-third have physical ailments with some degree of emotional involvement.

The pieces were falling into place. There was an awareness of the magnitude of the mental-illness problem. There was concern about the number of sufferers from mental illnesses. There was dissatisfaction with the overcrowded condition of many of our mental hospitals. New scientific facts were being uncovered and made available for application. More professionals were being produced. There were more and better training centers, and the concept of what constituted training was much broader than had formerly been the case. States and communities were significantly more concerned with what they could do to improve the mental health of all the people.

Finally, the hope stimulated by the psychoactive drugs had to a large extent become a reality. However, their appearance as agents for use in psychiatric conditions is an excellent example of serendipity. Clinicians seeking compounds which would be effective in other conditions found that some had an interesting side effect. They calmed the anxious patient without dulling his senses or narcotizing him.

In the United States investigators were studying *Rauwolfia serpentina*, or Indian Snake Root, for its hypotensive properties. They found that it also had a tranquilizing effect on the patients to whom it was given. In France physicians observed that patients awaiting surgery if given a "cocktail" containing the synthesized drug chlorpromazine to help potentiate the effects of other sedatives grew less anxious about the impending operation although they were perfectly aware of their surroundings and the nature of the procedure to be performed.

The advent of these drugs was historic and revolutionary. During the early days of reserpine, the *rauwolfia* derivative, and chlorpromazine, the synthetic, they were hailed as the answer to the problems of nearly all mental illness—they were the panacea, and, to the more enthusiastic, they were the means by which most if not all of the previous forms of treatment could be eliminated and mental illnesses could be eradicated. The popular press was filled with dramatic examples of work done with the drugs.

There was considerable justification for much of this enthusiasm. While they were not by any means the answer to all the problems of mental illness, these substances did provide the necessary ingredients for the solution of many of them. They did not replace all former methods of treatment, but some procedures were no longer employed as freely as before, some were discontinued in most places, and certainly the whole treatment routine, both in and out of hospitals, was modified.

Probably the most dramatic aspect of the new drugs was the way they worked. Unlike the barbiturates and other drugs that had been used to quiet patients in the years before, the tranquilizers did not produce sedation. Rather, they seemed to attack hostility, anxiety, and disorganized and unacceptable behavior—in short, they calmed the patient while affecting little or not at all his awareness of what was going on around him. Some patients became more alert; many who had not been amenable to the usual forms of treatment were now able to participate in therapy and other activities.

These drugs and others which rapidly began to appear can rightly be credited with being the most significant single factor in bringing about the tremendous changes that have taken place in mental hospitals and their patients since 1955. Psychopharmacologic agents have been greatly responsible in reducing the resident populations of our mental hospitals, not only because of their effect on the hospitalized patient but also because patients could be maintained on these drugs out of the hospital. Many patients who formerly had not been offered psychotherapy because of their disturbed condition when placed on the appropriate drug were able to benefit by this and other procedures which could be effective in attacking the roots of their problem. This reversal marked the beginning of the end of the situation which had been prevalent since the beginning of mental hospitals, whereby more and more patients were admitted each year because of population increases and increasing utilization of the institutions, among other things, without an offsetting number of discharges, with the inevitable result that hospital populations grew more rapidly than the facilities to care for them.

A look at ten-year figures will give us some idea of the alarming rate at which resident populations of mental hospitals had risen.[1] Between 1946 and 1955 there was an annual average rise of 2.1 per cent, and the number of patients resident at the end of the year climbed to an all-time high of 558,922 in 1955. Since then, however, there has been a steady, uninterrupted drop in end-of-year figures. The decrease began in 1956, and at the end of 1964 the number of resident patients fell below 500,000 for the first time in 15 years. The 1964 figure of 490,754 is a 10.9 per cent decrease since 1956. All this has been happening in the face of rising admissions: 302,946 persons, the largest number in history, were admitted to mental hospitals in 1964.

The drugs have been a significant factor in bringing about profound changes in the structure and administration of the mental hospital itself. No longer is it necessary to keep patients behind locked doors. More and more the open hospital is coming into use, and in some states, such as New York, entire hospitals are now open. Because the patients are calm and can be cared for as any other ill individual, it has been possible to do many things to make the hospital more cheerful and livable. Draperies or curtains will now be found on windows; patients now can and do eat at small tables accommodating four or six; self-government programs have been instituted in a number of hospitals; flowers will be found in the rooms and the dining rooms will have a homelike appearance. All of this has been conducive to better treatment of patients by personnel, which in turn has meant greater motivation on the part of many patients toward recovery and earlier release.

Many patients on maintenance doses of the appropriate psychoactive drug spend at first a portion and eventually all of their time outside the hospital. As this concept took practical form there developed the day-care and night-care hospitals where patients who could be at home in the evenings would come during the day for such treatment as needed, or where patients who could work during the day would come at night for treatment and care. The spectrum of therapeutic and supporting services available to the patients was widening.

As the knowledge spread that psychiatric patients in the main were not the dangerous or disturbing influence that they had so long been thought to be, physicians and hospital administrators started experimenting with their hospitalization and treatment in general hospitals. It was quickly determined that they could be cared for satisfactorily and effectively in such surroundings and that in many cases their hospital stay could be shortened with a resulting reduction in cost to family and public and in loss of time from work. By 1964 more psychiatric patients were admitted to general hospitals than were admitted to public mental hospitals.[2]

As the facilities for the treatment of the mentally ill increased in number and variety and the promise for early recovery from appropriate treatment became bright, the feasibility of covering mental illnesses under health-insurance programs became apparent. In 1955 of the seventy-nine Blue Cross plans forty had no significant provision for psychiatric coverage in their basic certificates which cover hospital care. Now the picture is quite different: of the plans in operation in the United States only a small percentage either exclude coverage for mental illnesses under their most widely held group certificate or permit it only under a special rider. These plans account for less than 5 per cent of Blue Cross membership. All other plans provide some mental-illness benefits.

In addition to basic hospitalization policies, many insurance carriers offer a type of coverage variously called major medical, extended benefits, or prolonged illness. This type of coverage, which is the fastest-growing type of health insurance in the United States, is subject to a deductible co-insurance (in which the patient pays a percentage of the bill) and a maximum-dollar limit. It provides benefits for most kinds of psychiatric-care expenses prescribed by a physician, including treatment in and out of the hospital, X-rays, prescriptions, and others. In 1963 a total of forty-eight Blue Cross plans included mental illnesses when offering extended benefits and/or major medical or prolonged illness coverage, in some cases with the participation of Blue Shield.[3]

Commercial insurance-company coverage for inhospital benefits under group policies is usually the same for mental and emotional disorders as for other conditions. This is not standard for policies issued to individuals. Group policies account for about 63 per cent of all health insurance written by commercial insurance companies. With regard to major medical policies most commercial companies writing such policies include coverage for mental conditions, but on a more restrictive basis than for physical illness. A large number of policies issued have a 50 per cent co-insurance feature for out-of-hospital care instead of the customary 75 to 80 per cent; some policies provide coverage only when the covered person is totally disabled, and some place a limitation on the total dollar coverage and the number of visits per illness. The Health Insurance Institute, whose members write 80 per cent of all commercial company health insurance, made a study of major medical group coverage in 1961 which showed that all but 9 per cent of the persons covered by a major medical plan had some coverage for mental and emotional disorders.

When the facts concerning health insurance for psychiatric illness are added to the other evidence of progress listed above, all of which bring greater promise of recovery to the mentally ill, it is small wonder that the demand for adequate psychiatric services has become an insistent one.

All these things mean that more and more, as time goes by, all physicians, not only psychiatrists, will be expected to cope with many of the manifestations of mental illnesses. It might be said parenthetically here that with the increasing complexity of medicine, the acquisition of new knowledge, and the development of new specialized techniques this same situation will exist in many other specialties. There is imperative need for a family-type physician with whom the family can first make contact for medical assistance or for advice. If such a physician is not available there should be some arrangement which will make possible the comprehensive knowledge of the health history and health status of all members of the family. Any specialized diagnostic or treatment services which the patient would require could be obtained through referral from the family physician when these were beyond his skill or experience; and upon completion of the specialized studies or treatment the patient would be referred back to this physician, who would serve as primary contact. This means, of course, more training in breadth and depth for the family physician.

Considering now the implications of such a plan for the field of psychiatry, this primary-contact physician, in order to fulfill his responsibilities to his patients, must have more than a superficial knowledge of the principles of psychiatry; he must know when to consult with a psychiatrist; conversely, the psychiatrist must be available when needed; and the family physician must be able to treat his patient in a facility such as a general hospital or a mental health center which is available both to him and to the psychiatrist.

This type of close collaboration between psychiatrist and other physicians is occurring more and more often over the country, and has led in recent years to a training program under the aegis of the National Institute of Mental Health which is flexible, inclusive, and designed to contribute to the pattern of medical care just described. The important aspects of the program are psychiatric training for nonpsychiatric residents and interns, psychiatric training for physicians in practice who want to broaden their knowledge in this field but do not intend to practice psychiatry as a specialty, and special short-term postgraduate education and training for nonpsychiatric physicians.

The first type of training is to add to the psychiatric knowledge of a physician, beyond what he would otherwise receive during his internship and residency. As a medical student he received training in psychiatry and as a physician in practice he can take postgraduate courses in this area of medicine. During the internship and residency period, however, he has all too often had inadequate access to psychiatric instruction. This type of training is designed to give him that access.

The Institute's program of support for physicians who wish to broaden their psychiatric understanding will provide full-time support for a course of study ranging from six months to a year. The postgraduate education and training in the form of lectures, seminars, case demonstrations, and conferences takes place in hospitals, clinics, medical schools, medical and psychiatric societies, and other institutions. This has proved to be one of the most popular forms of training undertaken.

The importance of such training is borne out when one considers the fact that, as stated earlier, no matter how many professional mental health workers are trained in the future there can never be, in the normal course of events, enough trained to cope with the problem if they only are to bear the responsibility. The Joint Commission report was quite correct when it said that increased and improved facilities mean increased awareness on the part of the public, which in turn will result in demands much greater than the professionals in the field can possibly meet.

This shortage, coupled with the growing psychiatric proficiency of nonpsychiatric physicians, the efficacy of the psychiatric drugs, and the increasing numbers of people being treated in nonpsychiatric settings, are the factors that led to the new program which has been the culmination of all we have discussed here—the program which is in reality the promise of what tomorrow holds for the mentally ill.

That program had its beginnings in the minds of many people. By the 1960s more knowledge was available than was being put to use. This knowledge properly applied would make it possible to attack the problem at its source: the patient in his home community. As pointed out previously, the home community is where people live and to which they must adjust. It is in the community that the mentally ill become sick and it is to the community that they return if they recover. As appropriate services are provided in the patient's home community, a number of very desirable goals will be achieved. First, of course, the patient will be treated where he lives. This will mean earlier attention and, hopefully, a shortening of the length of illness thereby. Second, he will be treated by skilled personnel who know well the social and cultural milieu in which he lives and in which he became ill. Third, as treatment for mental illnesses becomes a part of the community medical picture, much of the stigma of mental illness will disappear. Fourth, less stigma, shortened treatment, better prognosis, and treatment in the community all will contribute to more equitable and intelligent consideration by third-party payment plans.

All of this will make possible the achievement of another objective, which has been at the heart of the mental health movement since Clifford Beers founded the National Committee for Mental Hygiene. A mental hospital can now become a specialized facility of excellence for the treatment and rehabilitation of very difficult or complicated psychiatric cases. Here will be found the most skillful specialists, and they will be working in a setting which will provide those facilities and personnel necessary to assure the best possible outcome for patients under their care. Hope and expectation of recovery will be the atmosphere of this centralized facility. Never again will there be the old sights and scenes of the state hospital which so many of us remember. That state hospital as we knew, even as many are today, will disappear, and quite possibly within a quarter of a century.

This, then, is the concept of the comprehensive community mental health center. This concept is not the product of one or even a few minds. The Joint Commission on Mental Illness and Health recommended much of it; President Kennedy described the significant parts of it; and professionals and nonprofessionals alike in many areas of the country have been busily at work in clinics and hospitals which embody many elements of it. As we now look forward to the services a comprehensive community mental health center can render and the benefits the public should realize from it, we can predict the model center of the future. It is important that it be examined in some detail, for either it or something not dissimilar from it will be the primary resource of tomorrow. No doubt new developments of our fast-moving age will make what we see for tomorrow obsolete for the day after tomorrow. That is the wonder and excitement of living in our time. Nonetheless, at the risk of being considered an advocate of the obsolete almost before these words are preserved on the printed page, let us examine the model.

THE MODEL: At least six major areas of essential service will be included in a comprehensive community mental health program:

1. One area will, of course, be concerned with the diagnosis and treatment of mental and emotional disorders. This will embrace all of the various clinical services which are available, the therapeutic skills provided not only by the psychiatrists practicing in the community but by the other physicians as well. It will include outpatient facilities, psychiatric and others; psychiatric services in general hospitals; and specialized psychiatric facilities. Essential to the work of the center will be the case-finding services provided by schools, welfare agencies, and public health departments. For fullest effectiveness these agencies and individuals will work closely together.

2. A second essential area will include follow-up and rehabilitative services for persons returned from inpatient psychiatric care or under foster home or similar care.

3. A third component of tomorrow's comprehensive mental health program will be the provision of consultant services to schools, courts, public and private health and welfare agencies, and other gatekeepers of the community.

4. A fourth essential component will be public education. This includes public information and education programs which utilize the mass media as well as education activities conducted in smaller groups.

5. A fifth component of a mental health program must be community research—research to find answers to those problems that are at the root of mental and emotional disorders, and to try out and evaluate the effectiveness of new or unique mental health programs designed to meet the needs of the community. With the rapid acquisition of new knowledge, which will certainly not only continue but increase, communities will be testing and adapting new ideas to their particular situation and needs.

6. A sixth essential component of a comprehensive community mental health program will involve efforts to prevent mental illnesses. Prevention of mental illnesses implies not only the reduction of those factors which tend to produce mental and emotional disturbances, but also the provision of a climate in which each citizen has optimum opportunity for sustained creativity and responsible participation in the life of the community, and for the development of his particular potentialities as a human being.

Prevention as discussed thus far has had to do with activities which protect an individual or a population from a disease gaining a foothold in the first place. However, the ultimate goal is what was just said: the development of a climate conducive to better health, not just one in which disease finds difficulty in establishing itself. It is here that the mental health professional encounters problems in clearly defining his role. There are many elements which make up that salubrious climate which produces a more healthy, a more rugged, and a more resilient personality. For instance, an opportunity to achieve to the limit of one's potential is essential for optimum mental health and personality development. Frustration of this need in whole or in part, while not necessarily producing mental illness, often does produce individuals who utilize undesirable, if not unhealthy, mechanisms to work out a tolerable adjustment to life. Likewise, demands for more than one is capable of producing can have a similar effect. How far can the mental health center and its staff go, in the name of better mental health, to improve these conditions? How militant can one become and justify the activity on the basis of its being part of one's work and of the mission of the center? When do these activities belong in the realm of other professionals who, while having an interest in mental health, are by the nature of their work more concerned with other aspects of the community's problems? Should those concerned with preventive activities in the field of mental health, acknowledging the wide-ranging scope of their work and interest, attempt to be all things to all people, or even many things to most people? These questions have troubled all of us at one time or another, and they are raised here not to provide the opportunity to enunciate a neat answer—for one is not at hand—but to provoke further thinking.

Let us look further at the community mental health program which is coming into being. While the preventive aspect of the community program is extremely important, this must not be at the expense of the highest possible quality of care and treatment of people in hospitals. Appropriate and up-to-date inpatient care for mental disabilities must be strengthened and supported.

The development of facilities in the community for the care of patients needing hospitalization will become the rule, not the exception, and will come about in recognition of the need for close collaboration between community agencies and mental hospitals. It is necessary, therefore, that there be wide acceptance by both professionals and lay people of a frame of reference in which the mental hospitals are considered one facility and one resource, though not the sole facility or sole resource, in the whole chain of the community's armamentarium for dealing with mental and emotional illnesses.

The development of several new concepts has helped to point up the importance of energetic and interlocking community activity in order to promote mental health in the broadest possible sense. Some of these include the growing awareness of the importance of social relationships in the etiology and treatment of mental illnesses, the increased interest in the study of the mental hospital as a social institution, the recognition of the importance of a therapeutic environment in the hospital and the community, the introduction of public health concepts in the plans for treating and rehabilitating the mentally ill, and the recognition of the special needs of the aged, the alcoholic, and the mentally retarded.

Taking into account the existing state of mental health facilities in this country—and the essentiality of the components of a mental health program such as outlined above, the Center as envisioned will be a multiservice community facility designed to provide preventive services, early diagnosis, and treatment of mental illnesses on both an inpatient and outpatient basis, and to serve as a locus for the aftercare of discharged hospital patients. Thus it will encompass the following broad spectrum of services and programs:

A general diagnostic and evaluation service (pre-care);
An acute inpatient service;
An outpatient service;
A day-care service; a night-care service;
An emergency service available around-the-clock;
Rehabilitation services;
Consultation services;
Public information and education services;
Supervision of foster homes;
Research and training.

As one thinks of this array of services functioning as an interrelated whole in the community, one sees that continuity of care is possible, and that it has enormous advantages to the patient. As his needs change the patient in such a Center can move quickly to other appropriate services. Basically he is able to proceed from diagnosis to recovery and rehabilitation, and, if the need arises, back to treatment again.

Other essential elements of the program of tomorrow's Center will be consultative, educational, and information services to the public and to professional persons.

Skilled staff will be available to help physicians, teachers, clergymen, police and probation officers, lawyers, and social-agency personnel deal with the mental health problems of those they face in their day-to-day work.

Private physicians, including general practitioners, psychiatrists, and other medical specialists, must and will participate directly in the Community Mental Health Center operation.

Since each community in which these Centers will be located is unique, each Center will be unique. And it is expected that they will function under a variety of auspices: state, voluntary, municipal, private, within a group-practice arrangement, or any combination of these. Physically, it is expected that these Centers will exist under a variety of organizational arrangements and will provide a variety of services. For example, in one city it may be decided that the Center should be based at a general hospital. Since most of the large general hospitals—those with more than 500 beds—already have psychiatric facilities, facilities for day-care, night-care, and outpatient care will be added to fill out the comprehensive program.

In another community it is probable that the development of the Community Mental Health Center should start with an outpatient facility. Facilities for day-care, night-care, and inpatient services would be constructed with adequate office space for mental health staff to operate consultative and educational programs.

No matter what approach may be taken to the problem, one element will be essential: the community must be sincerely and deeply concerned for its fellow citizens.

If this is so there will be close cooperation between the various agencies and institutions and the Center. In this way, and only in this way, will the citizen needing help be optimally served. And this is the ultimate goal.

In achieving this goal there will need to be an open system of discussion and interaction, characterized by good will and good faith, and also by honest disagreement. Finally, this interchange will have to be characterized by flexibility, compromise, and continuing change.

The movement toward community-centered programs and activities has had a short but exceptionally active history. Probably the most important development has been the realization by general and specialized physicians that they can and should treat the emotional disturbances of their patients even when those disturbances are not accompanied by diagnosable physical illnesses.

This has added weight to the belief that retention of the mentally ill in the community is both feasible and practical, which in turn has made more urgent the development of the Community Mental Health Center concept. Far more broadly based than either the traditional outpatient clinic or the usual mental hospital, the Center will become the focus of future mental health activities within the community. Private physicians, including general practitioners, psychiatrists, and medical specialists, will participate directly in the Center operation. And the Center will for the first time provide a large proportion of private practitioners with treatment privileges in a facility directly and quickly available for care of their patients either full time or part time.

Among the most important features of the Center will

be the outpatient "walk-in" facilities and services discussed earlier. These will enable a person who recognizes that he requires help to find it quickly when he most needs it. Also among the vital features will be emergency psychiatric services, suicide prevention services, and home care and visits, including homemaker services.

Ideally in many localities the general hospital can serve as the nucleus for the Community Mental Health Center. More and more physicians and others, including the public, are recognizing that hospitalization for a mental disorder is similar to hospitalization for a physical disorder: the period of hospitalization need not be lengthy, and may be viewed as an episode in the disease process, not as the last recourse of the severely ill. We have learned that admission to a mental hospital often is not really the proper first step toward a cure. This process often merely prolongs the period of hospitalization, while treatment in a community facility such as the general hospital can tend to speed recovery.

This is the promise for tomorrow: Early recognition of mental and emotional disturbances; early availability of adequate treatment resources; financial protection against mental illnesses identical to that for physical illnesses; and removal of the stigma from mental and emotional disorders.

It is not a new story in the history of health and disease, for it was but a few years ago that the problem of tuberculosis was undergoing the same evolutionary process. Too little was known, too few resources were available, and the victim and his family were stigmatized. More recently epilepsy has gone through the same steps from fear and darkness into light. Now the mentally ill are coming into their own.

As I look back through the canyons of the years and the centuries to the early beginnings of hope for the mentally ill, I feel a sadness that it took so long for understanding and effective assistance to come to them. They have been much too long in the dark. But there is also within me a gladness that when light finally shone upon them I could see it and even have a part in it, for what I have seen and what I have lived through has been the telescoping into less than three decades of more real advances for the mentally ill than had been made during all the centuries before.

We are, I am convinced, well embarked upon a new era.

There exists a national mental health program which will involve, eventually, every town and hamlet in this country. It is a vibrant and viable entity. It is a program well calculated to involve us all and to utilize our energies and our skills.

President Kennedy knew the need for this involvement. He said: [4]

> We as a Nation have long neglected the mentally ill . . . This neglect must end, if our Nation is to live up to its own standards of compassion and dignity and achieve the maximum use of its manpower.
>
> This tradition of neglect must be replaced by forceful and far-reaching programs carried out at all levels of government, by private individuals and by State and local agencies in every part of the Union.
>
> We must act—

to bestow the full benefits of our society on those who suffer from mental disabilities;

to prevent the occurrence of mental illness . . . wherever and whenever possible;

to provide for early diagnosis and continuous and comprehensive care, in the community, of those suffering from these disorders;

to stimulate improvements in the level of care given the mentally disabled in our State and private institutions, and to reorient those programs to a community-centered approach;

to reduce, over a number of years, and by hundreds of thousands, the persons confined to these institutions;

to retain in, and return to, the community the mentally ill . . . and there to restore and revitalize their lives through better health programs and strengthened educational and rehabilitation services; and

to reinforce the will and capacity of our communities

to meet these problems, in order that the communities, in turn, can reinforce the will and capacity of individuals and individual families.

We must promote—to the best of our ability and by all possible and appropriate means—the mental and physical health of all our citizens. . . .

We have passed the point of no return in our long journey from a helter-skelter system of mental health services divorced from community life, without real grass-roots support, crippling to the patient and self-defeating in terms of the state of our medical and scientific knowledge.

Whatever difficulties we shall face in the future cannot be more difficult than those of the past—and the seeds which we have sown are now healthy sprouts. They are being nurtured by a concerned national community and give every promise of bearing good fruit. So, in this sixth decade of the twentieth century anno Domini, ends an era which had its beginnings in antiquity. In its place is the new day of hope and promise for the mentally ill. It would be wonderful again to be on the threshold of one's professional life and start from here. Yet, perhaps it is best for all concerned we cannot. For the generation now retiring from the wars was born and had its being in ignorance, prejudice, and adversity. These influences inevitably shaped its attitudes and reaction patterns. While it led us out of the wilderness of that day, now we need fresh forces not conditioned to unrelenting uphill struggle and not infrequent defeat, but to an equal place in the sun with all branches of medicine, and an attitude of assurance in success—now.

With this kind of leadership the walls of isolation and neglect which have cut the mentally ill off from their neighbors and friends and often from appropriate medical care will be destroyed.

For the children of Israel to achieve their destiny, they needed both a Moses to lead them to the Promised Land and Joshua to secure it for them and their children. In the Book of Joshua, Sixth Chapter, we read, "Joshua said to the people, shout, for the Lord hath given unto you the city . . . and the people shouted with a great shout, and the walls fell down flat."

In the field of mental health and illness, Joshua now enters and proceeds to center stage.

NOTES

I. TOWARD MENTAL HEALTH

1. Ralph H. Major, *A History of Medicine*, Charles C Thomas, Springfield, Illinois, 1954, p. 164.
2. James C. Coleman, *Abnormal Psychology and Modern Life*, Third Edition, Scott, Foresman and Company, Chicago, 1964, p. 28.
3. Major, *A History of Medicine*, p. 206.
4. Albert Deutsch, *The Mentally Ill in America*, Second Edition, Columbia University Press, New York, 1949, p. 8.
5. Public Health Service Publication, "Mental Illness and Its Treatment: Past and Present," No. 1345, U.S. Government Printing Office, Washington, D.C., 1963, p. 3.
6. Coleman, *Abnormal Psychology and Modern Life*, p. 27.
7. Deutsch, *The Mentally Ill in America*, p. 8.
8. Coleman, *Abnormal Psychology and Modern Life*, p. 28.
9. Major, *A History of Medicine*, pp. 217–18.
10. Major, *Ibid.*, p. 388.
11. Coleman, *Abnormal Psychology and Modern Life*, p. 30.
12. Coleman, *Ibid.*, p. 33.
13. Deutsch, *The Mentally Ill in America*, p. 18.
14. W. E. H. Lecky, *History of the Rise of the Spirit of Rationalism in Europe*, London, 1872, Vol. I, p. 82.
15. Deutsch, *The Mentally Ill in America*, p. 21.

16. Deutsch, *Ibid.*, p. 22.
17. Coleman, *Abnormal Psychology and Modern Life*, p. 33.
18. Deutsch, *The Mentally Ill in America*, p. 22.
19. Coleman, *Abnormal Psychology and Modern Life*, p. 37.
20. Deutsch, *The Mentally Ill in America*, p. 60.
21. Deutsch, *Ibid.*, p. 71.
22. Coleman, *Abnormal Psychology and Modern Life*, p. 39.
23. Deutsch, *The Mentally Ill in America*, pp. 92–95.
24. Public Health Service Publication, "Mental Illness and Its Treatment: Past and Present," p. 6.
25. Deutsch, *The Mentally Ill in America*, p. 158.
26. Nina Ridenhour, *Mental Health in the United States*, Harvard University Press, Cambridge, 1961, p. 28.

II. AN AROUSED AMERICA

1. William C. Menninger, *Psychiatry in a Troubled World*, Macmillan, 1948, p. 282.
2. P. Lemkau, C. Tietze, and M. Cooper, "Mental Hygiene Problems in an Urban District," *Mental Hygiene*, 25:624–46 (1941); 26:100–119, 275–88 (1942); 27:279–99 (1943).
3. W. F. Roth and F. H. Luton, "The Mental Health Program in Tennessee. I. Description of the Original Study Program. II. Statistical Report of a Psychiatric Survey in a Rural County," *American Journal of Psychiatry*, 99:662–65, 666–75 (1943).
4. National Institute of Mental Health, "Patients in Mental Institutions." Published Annually, U.S. Government Printing Office, Washington, D.C.
5. Clifford W. Beers, *A Mind That Found Itself*, New York, Doubleday, 1908.

6. Jeanne L. Brand, "The National Mental Health Act of 1946: A Retrospect," *Bulletin of the History of Medicine,* XXXIX, No. 3, May–June, 1965, pp. 231–45.

7. Hearings before a Subcommittee of the Committee on Interstate and Foreign Commerce, House of Representatives, 79th Congress, First Session, on H.R. 2550, National Neuropsychiatric Act, September 18–19–21, 1945. U.S. Government Printing Office, Washington, D.C., 1945.

III. THE OPENING DOOR

1. George W. Albee, *Mental Health Manpower Trends.* No. 3 of Monograph Series issued under auspices of The Joint Commission on Mental Illness and Health, Basic Books, New York, 1959.

2. *Public Law 182,* U.S. Congress, 1955.

3. Jack R. Ewalt, editor, *Action for Mental Health,* The Final Report of the Joint Commission on Mental Illness and Health, Basic Books, New York, 1961.

4. Robert H. Felix, *The New Era: Promises and Problems,* The National Institute of Mental Health, 1964.

5. John F. Kennedy, Message from the President of the United States Relative to Mental Illness and Mental Retardation, U.S. Government Printing Office, Washington, D.C., 1963.

6. *Public Law 88-164,* U.S. Congress, 1963.

7. *Public Law 89-105,* U.S. Congress, 1965.

IV. TOMORROW'S PROMISE

1. Morton Kramer, Chief, Biometrics Branch, National Institute of Mental Health, Public Health Service, Department of Health, Education, and Welfare. Personal communication.

2. National Institute of Mental Health, "Patients in Mental Institutions." Published Annually, U.S. Government Printing Office, Washington, D.C.

3. Public Health Service Publication, "Improving Mental Health Insurance Coverage," No. 1253, U.S. Government Printing Office, Washington, D.C., 1965.

4. John F. Kennedy, Message from the President of the United States Relative to Mental Illness and Mental Retardation, U.S. Government Printing Office, Washington, D.C., 1963.